Images of America
Around Bellows Falls
Rockingham, Westminster, and Saxtons River

IMAGES
of America

AROUND BELLOWS FALLS
ROCKINGHAM, WESTMINSTER, AND SAXTONS RIVER

Anne L. Collins, Virginia Lisai,
and Louise Luring

Copyright © 2002 by Anne L. Collins, Virginia Lisai, and Louise Luring
ISBN 978-0-7385-1033-0

Published by Arcadia Publishing
Charleston, South Carolina

Printed in the United States of America

Library of Congress Catalog Card Number: 2002103050

For all general information contact Arcadia Publishing at:
Telephone 843-853-2070
Fax 843-853-0044
E-mail sales@arcadiapublishing.com
For customer service and orders:
Toll-Free 1-888-313-2665

Visit us on the Internet at www.arcadiapublishing.com

Contents

Acknowledgments   6

Introduction   7

1. Bellows Falls   9

2. Westminster   61

3. Saxtons River   91

ACKNOWLEDGMENTS

Anne L. Collins would like to thank a number of individuals who made this book possible, particularly Virginia Lisai and Louise Luring. Thanks go to the members of the board at the Rockingham Free Public Library for the use of the library's photographs and to Patty Mark for helping to organize the photographs. A special acknowledgment goes to Ed Underhill, who passed away on Christmas Day 2001. Ed worked for the fire department as its photographer and was also a member of the Connecticut Valley Camera Club.

Virginia Lisai would like to thank Bob Haas and Richard Michelman for sharing their private photograph and postcard collections. Thanks also go to Alice Caggiano for her invaluable research and editing. The balance of photographs and cards came from the Westminster Historical Society.

Louise Luring would like to thank Tamra Mooney, the archivist at Vermont Academy, for her assistance. Also, thanks go to the Saxtons River Historical Society for the contribution of the photographs.

Introduction

Located along the western shore of the Connecticut River between Brattleboro and Springfield is an area alive with rich history—Rockingham Township, which includes Bellows Falls, Saxtons River, and the town of Westminster. Still noted for its rich farmland and agricultural products, the area also retains remnants of the industries that once thrived in its villages. The geography is representative of the forces of the Ice Age, which gouged the valley and created the waterfalls and terraces unique to this part of the river valley.

As early as 1724, Fort Dummer protected early settlers on the river in what is now Brattleboro. By 1727, the fort called No. 4 in Charlestown, New Hampshire, had been established. However, frequent attacks by Native Americans prevented any real settlement of towns. In 1752, residents persevered and established clearings and houses in Rockingham and Westminster on the higher elevations near the river.

Near the northern boundary of Rockingham is the Williams River, which was named for Rev. John Williams, who was taken hostage by Native Americans at Deerfield, Massachusetts. He preached a sermon to his fellow captives at the point where the river empties into the Connecticut River. South on the Connecticut is the Great Falls, once a sacred area to Native Americans, who left carvings in the rocks below the falls. The Saxtons River, which begins in Grafton, flows through the villages of Cambridgeport and Saxtons River and converges with the Connecticut River about a mile below the falls. Many mills lined the riverbanks, taking advantage of the large lumber supply upstream and the waterpower. These mills produced wool, tin, paper, and wooden products. The small settlements along these rivers became the self-sufficient villages of Bellows Falls, Bartonsville, Brockways Mills, Cambridgeport, Saxtons River, and Gageville. Until as recently as 1980, paper mills were in operation in Bellows Falls.

Just below the Great Falls, the first bridge across the Connecticut River was built by Col. Enoch Hale in 1785. It was 360 feet in length and built solely at his expense. In order to provide access to the upper river by boat, a canal was dug to the west of the falls in 1791 by the Bellows Falls Canal Company; it was the first such canal in the country. It was provided with locks and was in use for many years. With the advent of the railroad in the mid-1800s, the river was no longer an economical form of transportation and the canal fell into disuse. The great volume of water that was channeled through the canal continued to power many mills. Today, the canal still provides water to the electric power plant below the falls. A fish ladder was built to bypass the power turbines, allowing native salmon and shad a way to travel upstream and spawn.

The railroad into the area was built between 1849 and 1851. Bellows Falls became a hub for trains from Boston; Hartford, Connecticut; and Burlington. Many Irish immigrants worked as laborers laying the track. They later settled nearby to raise their families.

Quite a few famous and some infamous men and women have been attracted to the area. During the years when women were not allowed to own property or take an active part in the business world, there came to Bellows Falls a woman who would become notorious for amassing millions. She was born in New Bedford, Massachusetts, on November 21, 1834, with the name Hetty Howland. She met and married Edward Green of Bellows Falls. Hetty Green became known as the Witch of Wall Street, not only because of her amazing wizardry at making money on the stock market, but also because of her reputed miserable treatment of her children and husband.

Stephen Row Bradley, one of Westminster's early town clerks, lived along King's Highway in Westminster Village. It was also here that Ethan Allen met and married his second wife. In Westminster's original charter, Col. Josiah Willard was the largest landowner. He never settled in Westminster, but many of his descendants have lived and prospered here. Perhaps the most famous of these were Joseph and Henry Willard, who became owners of the Willard Hotel in Washington, D.C.

Rev. Charles Albert Dickinson, born in Westminster in 1849, was a noted minister in Maine and Massachusetts. He was responsible for establishing the Kurn Hattin Homes on the hill overlooking Westminster Village. There, he arranged for the care of countless numbers of boys and girls who could not care for themselves. The home and school continue today.

In the village of Saxtons River, Vermont Academy was founded in 1876 to educate the sons of Baptist missionaries. The school was first located in a large house. Soon, however, Jones Hall was built on a terrace overlooking the village. Today, 250 students from around the world attend the private secondary school.

Route 5, running northward from Connecticut to the Canadian border, was a favorite route for tourists, leaf-peepers, and skiers on their way to the mountains. Many businesses catered to the traffic, selling souvenirs and offering lodging and refreshment. Most of these small businesses closed when they were bypassed with the creation of Interstate 91 in 1960.

While Westminster and Rockingham are noted for their Federal-style homes, Bellows Falls is proud of its large Victorian houses with varied painted exteriors. A section of Bellows Falls has been included on the National Register of Historic Places. The area surrounding King's Highway in Westminster village is listed on the same register.

Full of community spirit, the area boasts many celebrations. Saxtons River has become known for its small-town Fourth of July parade and activities; Bellows Falls is famous for its Alumni Parade, with one of the highest percentage of participants returning to celebrate. Old Home Days is an August celebration featuring community events and the largest fireworks display in the area. The celebration culminates with an annual pilgrimage to Vermont's oldest public building, the 1787 Rockingham Meeting House, designated a National Historic Site in 2000.

One

Bellows Falls

The Connecticut River flows on the eastern side of Bellows Falls and is the village's entire boundary on the east. In earlier times, before Bellows Falls was settled, Native Americans would fish, shad and salmon being very plentiful. Later, larger flat boats came into use to transport freight to the important areas of the falls, going to and from Hartford, Connecticut, and Springfield, Massachusetts. This was the occupation of the first citizens of this area, along with fishing for salmon and shad.

Rockingham was chartered in December 1752 under the authority of King George II of England. The name Rockingham was chosen by Governor Wentworth in honor of the Marquis of Rockingham, Charles Watson Wentworth, who was the governor's relative and was the first lord of the treasury and prime minister of England in 1765–1766 and again in later years.

The Rockingham Meeting House was built by the town of Rockingham in 1787. It was used for religious and civil affairs and was a place of worship for 42 years. The town meetings were held there until 1869. Baptists, Congregationalists, and Universalists all used the building for worship services. The meetinghouse became a National Historic Site on May 16, 2000.

Bellows Falls is the principal village in the town of Rockingham. The village was settled in 1792, one year after construction on the canal had begun. The Bellows Falls Canal Company and John Atkinson built the canal, which was financed totally by England. Because of obstacles met along the way, the canal could not be used until 1802. It was one of six navigation canals built along the Connecticut River during this time.

Bellows Falls was known as a mill town. The first paper mill came in 1802, built by Bill Blake. When the railroad came into town, Bellows Falls became an important junction for the paper industry. It encouraged growth in business, as companies would move to a town that had good rail service. The manufacturing of paper was the leading industry of Bellows Falls from the time of the first paper mill until the 1960s and 1970s.

The National Park Service announced that the Bellows Falls Neighborhood District was officially entered on the National Register of Historic Places on January 17, 2002.

December 28, 2002, marks the 250th anniversary of the town of Rockingham. This celebration will last through November 2003.

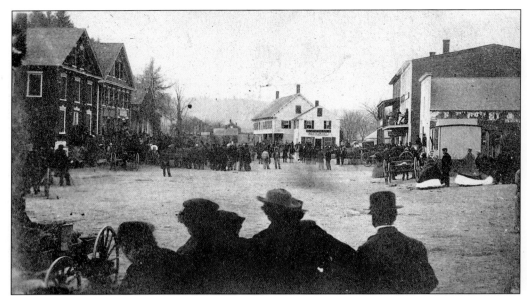

In the 1860s, there were two large fires in the square, one on March 14, 1860, in which the cost of the damage was estimated at $50,000, and another on July 28, 1868, seen here. This fire burned a large frame building, which was owned by O.F. Woods as a hotel, drugstore, and book store. The fire also destroyed the King Block and a building just south of it, a J.C. Goodwin & Company harness shop. (Courtesy of the Rockingham Free Public Library.)

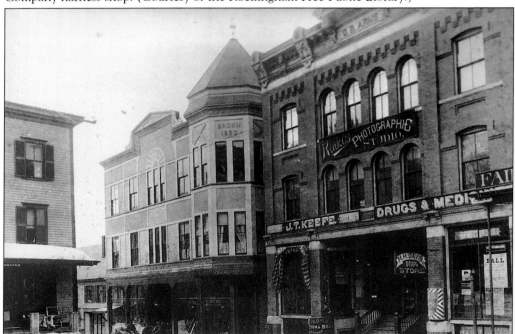

Seen here is the Brown Block, erected by Amos Brown in 1890 on the east side of Canal Street. Brown lived on Henry Street for 27 years. He held many public offices and was considered a man with excellent judgment who was respected for his good advice. (Courtesy of the Rockingham Free Public Library.)

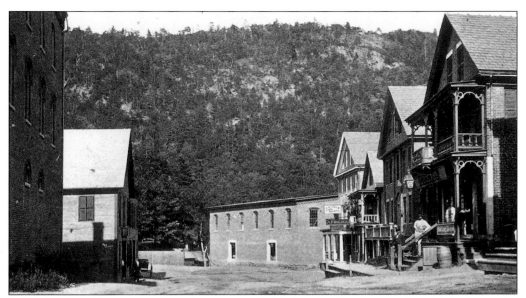

Fall Mountain Paper is seen in the center of this late-1800s photograph, which shows the south end of the square. Fall Mountain Paper derived from a merging of the Bellows Falls Paper Company, New England Pulp, William Russell & Son, and Willard Russell in 1872. William Russell was the owner. In 1898, Fall Mountain Paper was merged into the International Paper Company. (Courtesy of the Rockingham Free Public Library.)

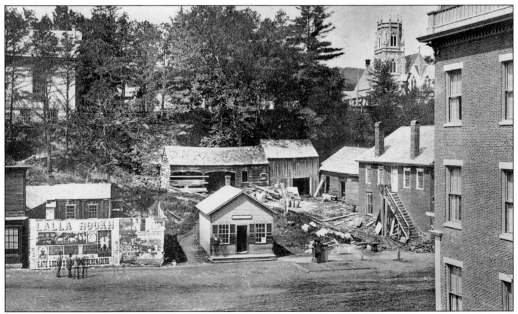

Seen here is the west side of the square in 1840s. John W. Moore became postmaster on April 24, 1841, and the post office was moved into his printing office just north of the Mansion House. In 1843, the post office was moved into the hotel for only a few months by William R. Williams. Moore was appointed again as postmaster and moved the post office back to his printing office in 1843. (Courtesy of the Rockingham Free Public Library.)

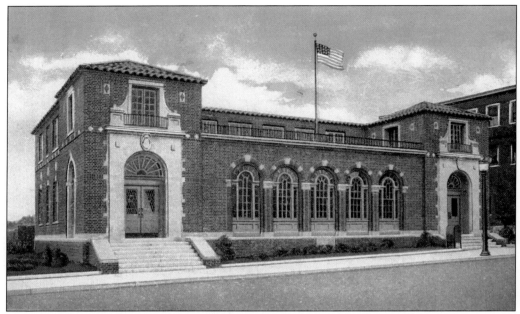

The post office seen here was built in 1930 on Bridge Street. (Author's collection.)

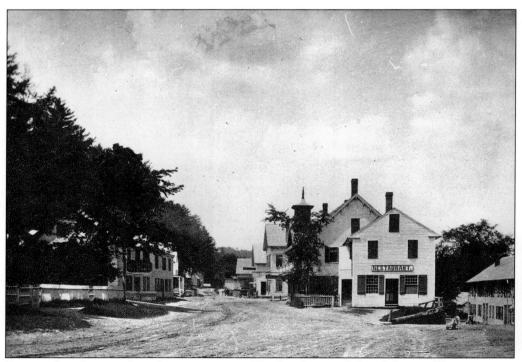

Seen in this photograph is the intersection of Rockingham and Canal Streets. The restaurant shown was owned by E.E. Dewey. (Courtesy of the Rockingham Free Public Library.)

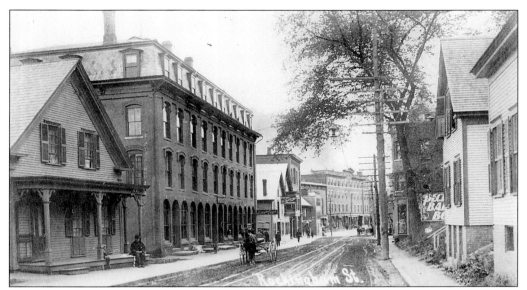

In this view of Rockingham Street, looking south, the Hotel Rockingham is on the left. The Hotel Rockingham was owned by Leverett T. Lovell II. Lovell erected the building, which was designed for use as a hotel, c. 1883. However, the building was rented out as store and office space. It was refurbished, to be used as a hotel, c. 1893. The building had about 50 rooms, with steam heat and electric lighting. It is now called the Canal House. (Courtesy of the Rockingham Free Public Library.)

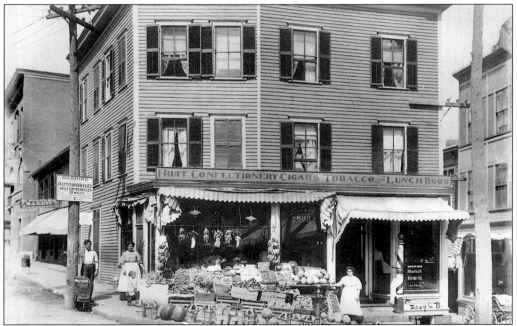

Baldasaro's fruit market, on Rockingham Street on north end of the square, was owned by Pasquale Baldasaro in the early 1900s. Baldasaro hung bunches of bananas outside, as well as baskets of oranges, apples, watermelons, and coconuts. (Courtesy of the Rockingham Free Public Library.)

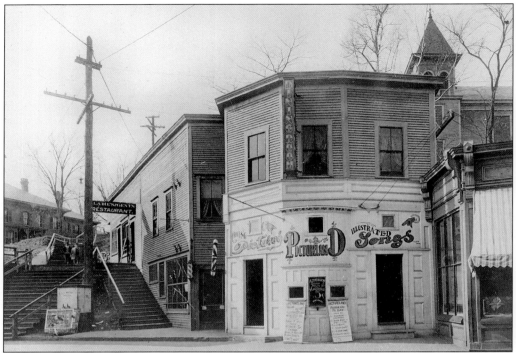

The Pictureland theater was located at the foot of the 44 steps. Mrs. Stillwell's millinery shop is to the right. Her shop later became Whelan Drug. (Courtesy of the Rockingham Free Public Library.)

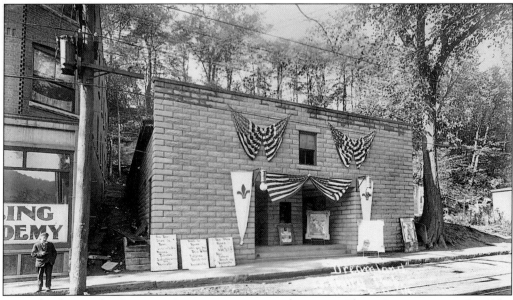

Dreamland, now the American Legion, was organized in 1919. This is Pierce-Lawton Post No. 37, named in honor William G. Pierce and Paul and Fred Lawton, who were World War I veterans. (Courtesy of the Rockingham Free Public Library.)

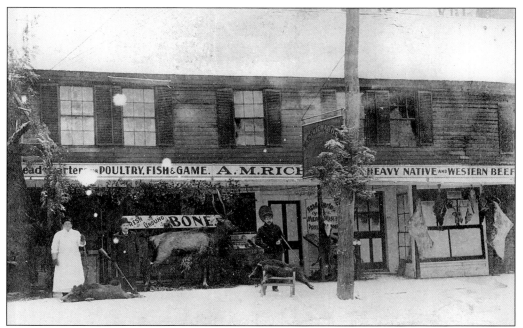

F.W. Richards started a meat business near the Commercial House c. 1896. He had a good business. After he died, his brothers A.M. and H.S. Richards bought the business. They kept all kinds of smoked and salted meats, which were both local and western beef. Before the Richards brothers bought this building, it was known as the Morgan Tavern. (Courtesy of the Rockingham Free Public Library.)

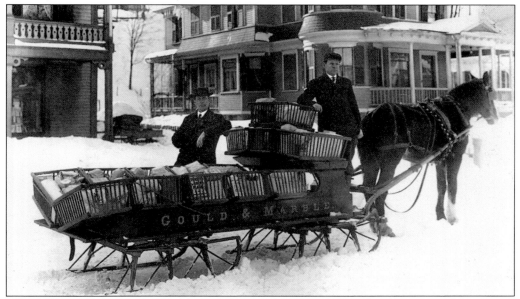

Gould & Marble was located at the south end of town. The owners were Ernest Gould and Leon Marble. They bought the business from Charles Underhill. They had a delivery sleigh that was used to deliver orders that had been taken in the morning. The orders were delivered before dinnertime. (Courtesy of the Rockingham Free Public Library.)

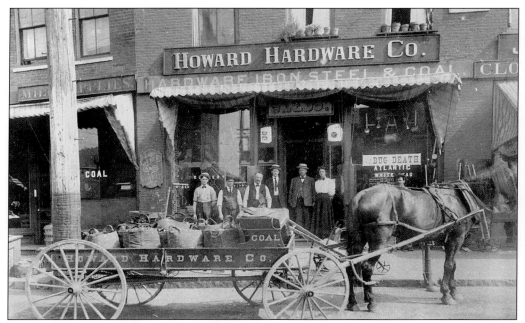

Seen here is Howard Hardware, located at the south end of the square, with its delivery wagon. Coal was put into canvas bags and delivered by hand. (Courtesy of the Rockingham Free Public Library.)

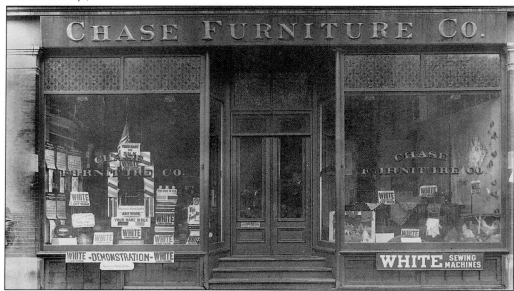

Chase Furniture, managed by Clark Chase, was located in this 1871 building, which was built by Chase and Frank Hadley. The store was purchased in 1878 by James T. Keefe. An undertaking business, located on the second floor, was established in 1880. Keefe operated the business until his death in 1911. In 1912, J.J. Fenton bought the stock and business, including the undertaking business. J.C. Hennessey, who had been an employee of Fenton, became his partner. After J.J. Fenton died, J.C. Hennessey ran the store and the undertaking business. (Courtesy of the Rockingham Free Public Library.)

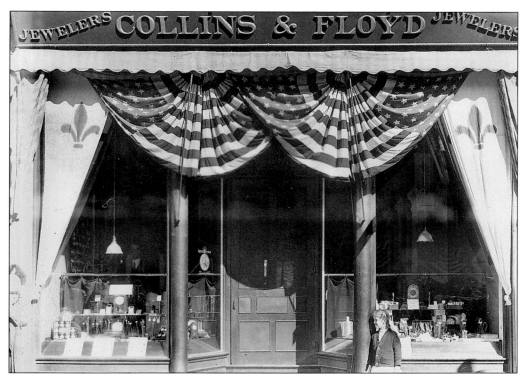

This store was originally owned by M.D. Jackson, who sold it to W.J. Eaton. Eaton sold the store to Collins & Floyd Jewelers in 1911. N.O. Cote worked for Collins & Floyd Jewelers in 1920. In 1926, Cote opened his own store in Windsor. Cote purchased this store in 1935 and worked there until his death in 1957. It was known as Cote Jewelers. (Courtesy of the Rockingham Free Public Library.)

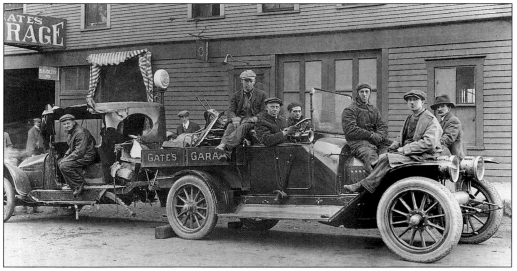

A.S. Gates was a wallpaper hanger, hardwood finisher, and a mechanic. He owned Gates Garage, which was a repository of bicycles and carried a large stock of wheels and sundries. He also kept cars in storage for people. (Courtesy of the Rockingham Free Public Library)

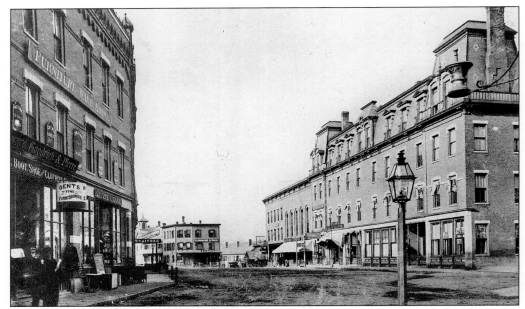

This view of the east side of the square looks north in the early 1800s. The Towns Hotel, built in 1871 by C.W. Towns, is on the right. It was destroyed by fire in 1899. When it was remodeled, a fourth story was added. It kept its name until 1902, when F.F. Shepard bought it and renamed it the Hotel Windham. The building burned again in 1912, and then again in 1932. (Courtesy of the Rockingham Free Public Library.)

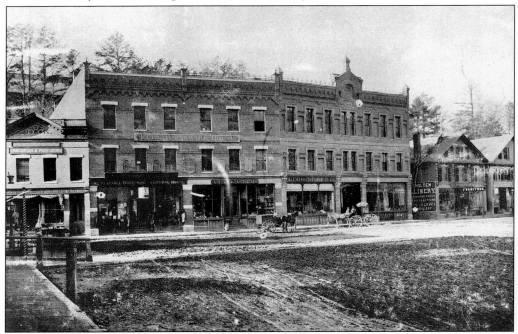

The Centennial Block was built in 1875. Chase Furniture was located in this building. Before the building was erected, the Mansion House was located here. (Courtesy of the Rockingham Free Public Library.)

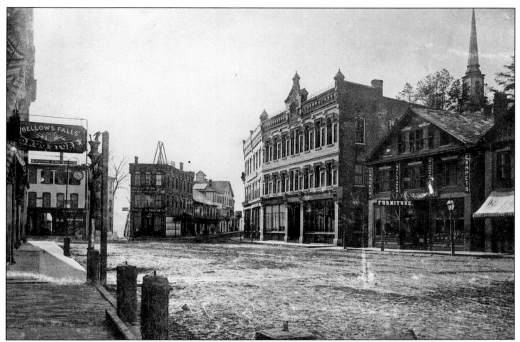

This 1800s view, looking south, shows the west side of the square. Note the hitching posts on the left. The last hitching post was kept intact in front of Howard Hardware, after 1919, for occasional use by horse travelers. (Courtesy of the Rockingham Free Public Library.)

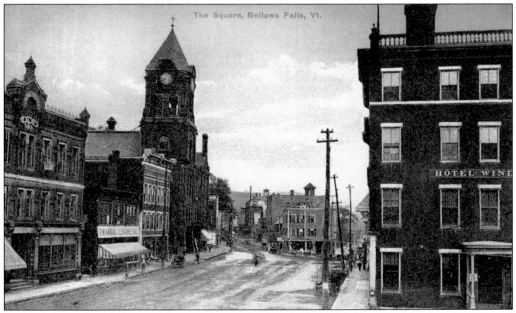

In the summer of 1869, a frame engine house, hall, and village building were built, which served the town for all its purposes until 1903. In later years, the voters held meetings in the town hall, which was built in 1887 and burned in 1925. Another town hall was built. Each side of the square has changed dramatically over the years. (Author's collection.)

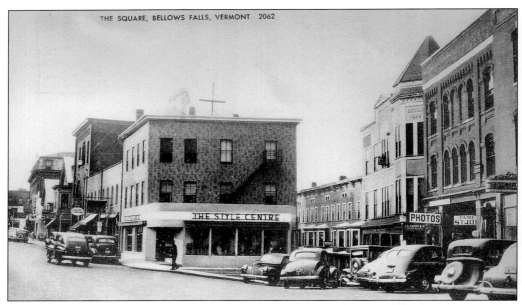

In this 1940s view of the square is the Style Centre, which opened for business in 1941. The Exner Block is to the right. The block now serves as apartments and studios for artists. Sovernet, a local Internet service provider, now occupies the building where the Style Centre was. (Author's collection.)

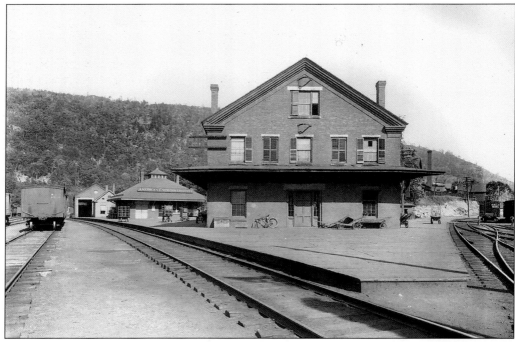

The first railroad to reach Bellows Falls was the Cheshire—part of the Fitchburg division of the Boston & Maine—c. 1849. This station was a junction of the main lines to the north and west from Boston and New York. The depot was a flurry of activity every day. (Courtesy of Ed Underhill.)

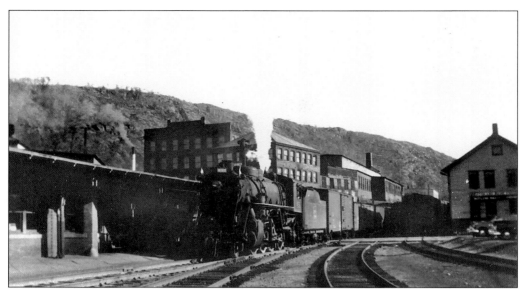

This early-1930s view of the Bellows Falls station shows a freight train coming in. By the 20th century, all of the through routes out of Bellows Falls, with the exception of the Rutland Railroad, were controlled by the Boston & Maine Railroad. (Courtesy of Ed Underhill.)

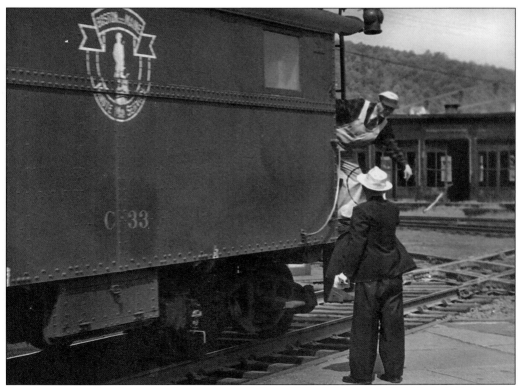

Seen here is a train departing the station in Bellows Falls. (Courtesy of Ed Underhill.)

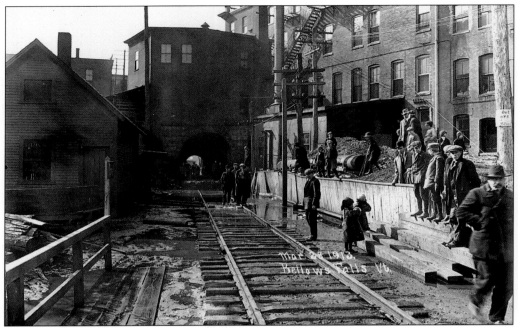

This train tunnel runs under the square, underneath several businesses, and is about 400 feet in length. It was built in 1850 and opened direct line traffic from the upper valley. (Courtesy of the Rockingham Free Public Library.)

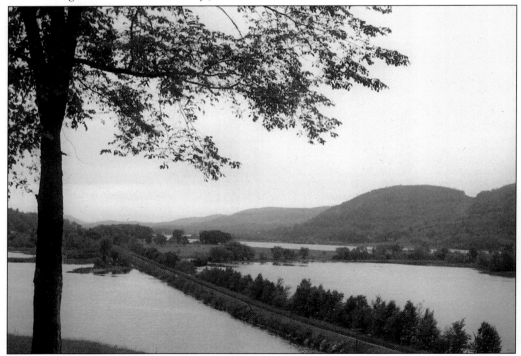

This is the setback that is located on the north side of town. The tracks are those of the Rutland Railroad, and the homes are along Route 5. (Courtesy of Ed Underhill.)

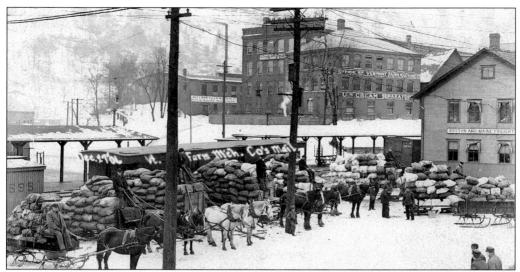

The Creamery & Vermont Farm Machine started out under the name of Hartford Sorghum Machine Company in 1868. In 1873, the name of was changed to the Vermont Farm Machine. The U.S. Cream Separator, beside the Vermont Farm Machine, was one of the largest manufacturers of dairy equipment in the world. One of the creations was the Cooley Creamer in 1877. In 1889, the Davis Swing Churn was an important manufactured item that was sent all over the world from Bellows Falls. Here, in the foreground, the mail is being collected. (Author's collection.)

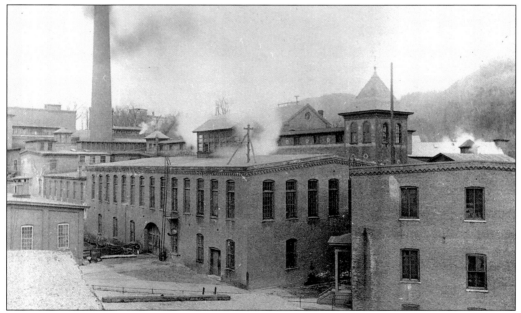

International Paper and Fall Mountain Paper merged in 1898. International Paper had mills at 31 locations throughout the country; it was the largest producer of paper and pulp in the world. The business was established by the Honorable William Russell of Lawrence, Massachusetts. He had two partners when he first came to Bellows Falls, but they stayed only a short time. In later years, A.N. Burbank became his partner. (Courtesy of the Rockingham Free Public Library.)

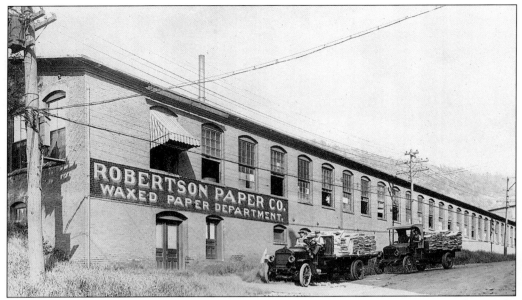

Seen here is the Robertson Paper Company. John Robertson and his son came to Bellows Falls in 1872; their paper mill was erected in 1881 on the site of what was then the John T. Moore & Son Paper Mill. In 1882, Moore and Robertson divided the business—Moore took the old mill, and Robertson took the new building that had been built on Island Street. (Courtesy of the Rockingham Free Public Library.)

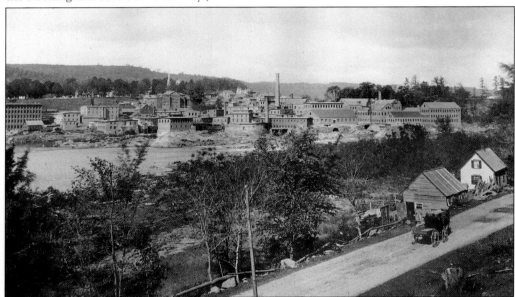

The first paper mill in Vermont was built in Bellows Falls in 1802 by Bill Blake. He had come from Alstead, New Hampshire, where he had built a paper mill in 1799. The mill he constructed in 1802 burned in 1812, so he built another, which was destroyed by fire in 1846. He did not rebuild again. No new paper mills were constructed until 1870. Paper manufacturing was the leading industry in Bellows Falls until the 1960s and 1970s. (Courtesy of the Rockingham Free Public Library.)

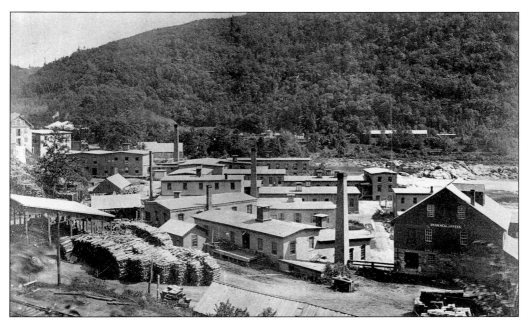

The Adams Grist Mill was erected by John Carey of England in 1831. It was managed by John Billing. For $1,000, Carey bought water privileges for the mill, using the canal for the waterpower. In 1875, Horace Adams bought the mill, and it stayed in the family until 1961. (Courtesy of the Rockingham Free Public Library.)

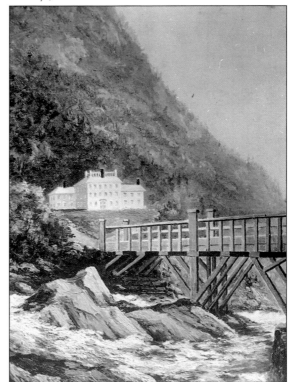

This covered bridge was built in 1785 by Enoch Hale under a special act of the New Hampshire legislature. The act enabled him to build and maintain a bridge over the Connecticut River. The bridge was used to cart freight from boats above and below the falls. In June 1804, the New Hampshire legislature implemented a toll for passing over the bridge. (Courtesy of the Rockingham Free Public Library.)

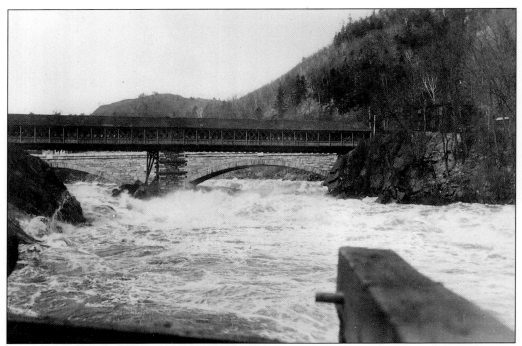

The Tucker Toll Bridge was built in 1840 by Samford Granger. It replaced the bridge that Enoch Hale built. Tucker himself used to collect the tolls from a gate on the New Hampshire side. Legend has it that he would sometimes give the day's tolls to his daughter for pin money. His daughter would sit at her window and count the passengers over the bridge. The Tucker Toll Bridge was razed in 1930. (Courtesy of the Rockingham Free Public Library.)

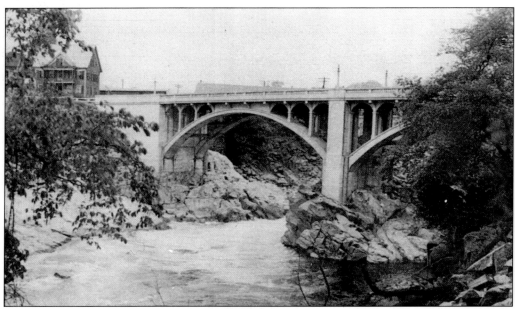

The Vilas Bridge replaced the Tucker Toll Bridge. It is an interstate bridge between Bellows Falls and Walpole, New Hampshire. (Author's collection.)

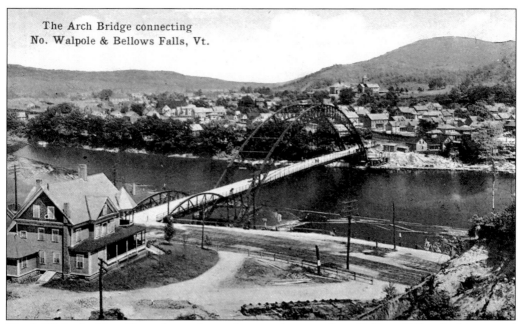

North Walpole, New Hampshire—located across the river from Bellows Falls—had increased in population by 1904, so a better highway bridge facility was needed. The town of Rockingham held a meeting on March 1, 1904, and it was decided that a new, steel arch bridge would be erected. The bridge was completed and was open to the public on March 20, 1905. The total cost of the bridge was $44,939. The bridge was razed in 1982. (Author's collection.)

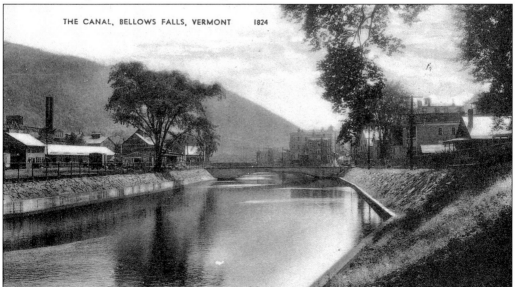

Construction on this canal was started in 1791 by the Bellows Falls Canal Company. The canal could not be used until 1802. Unforeseen problems occurred that stalled the building, and the cost was greater than expected by the projectors. John Atkinson invested money in the building of the canal, and Dr. William Page, a civil engineer, built it. The Connecticut River was the first river in the country to be improved by canals. (Author's collection.)

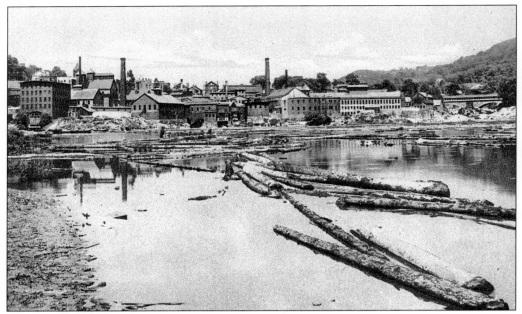

It has been said that logs for the English navy floated down the Connecticut River as early as 1732, before settlement of the area. (Author's collection.)

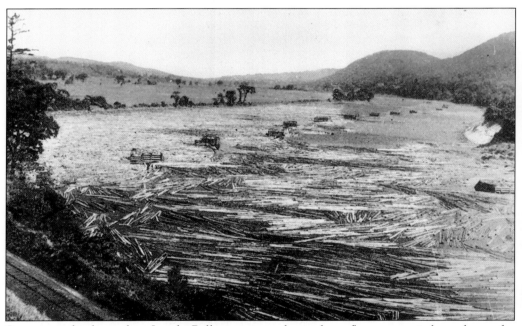

State records show that Josiah Bellows was authorized to float pine timbers down the Connecticut River, south of all dams and canals. He could do this at any time from April 20 to December 1, except for July and August. No timber could be put in the water above the Walpole Village bridge, and he could channel only his own timber down the river. Also, any timber deposited on land would belong to the landowner unless removed within 10 days. (Courtesy of the Rockingham Free Public Library.)

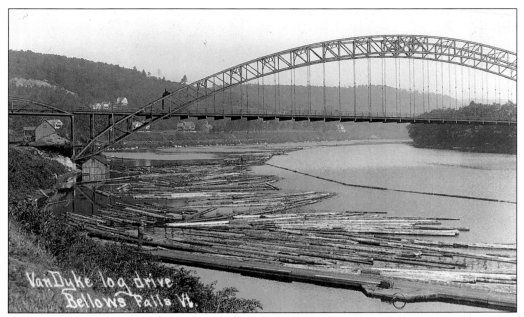

The Van Dyke Company had log drives that came through Bellows Falls in the early 1900s. In 1908, the Boat Club got an injunction against the Van Dyke Company to prevent the logs from filling the river and spoiling the club's fun on the river. The last log drive was in 1919. (Author's collection.)

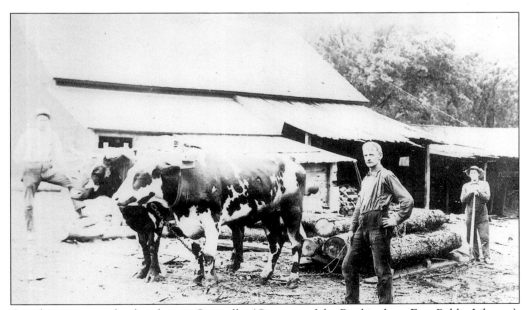

Seen here are oxen hauling logs in Gageville. (Courtesy of the Rockingham Free Public Library.)

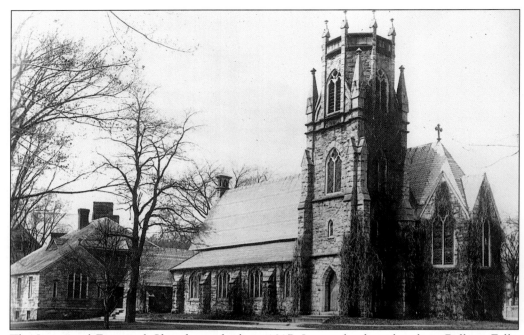

The Immanuel Episcopal Church was built in 1817. It was the first church in Bellows Falls. It was the only religious society organized in the 18th century in town. It is still in existence. Hetty Green is buried near the church. (Courtesy of the Rockingham Free Public Library.)

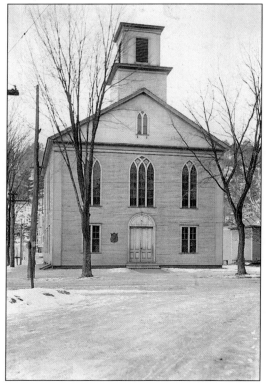

The Methodist Episcopal Church was built in 1836 and was organized by the first pastor, Rev. Elijah Mason. It was remodeled from 1880 to 1881 to accommodate social and vestry rooms on the first floor. The sanctuary was on the second floor. Additional improvements were made in 1900. The church building was sold to Fall Mountain Grange in 1942. It now houses the Meeting Waters YMCA. In 1934, the Methodists united with the already integrated Congregationalists and Universalists. (Courtesy of the Rockingham Free Public Library.)

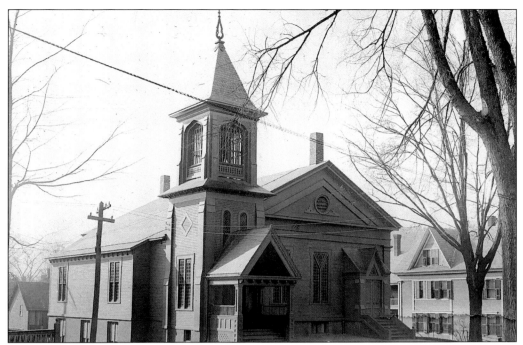

The Congregational church was built in 1851. It was the idea of Mary I. Walker and her husband, Charles I. Walker, who had moved to Bellows Falls from Saxtons River. It was called the First Congregational Society of Bellows Falls until 1889, when it became known as the Congregational Church. In 1928, the Universalists united with them, and now it is called the United Church of Bellows Falls. A new building was erected in 1984. (Courtesy of the Rockingham Free Public Library.)

The First Baptist Church was organized in 1854, and the building was erected in 1860. Baptisms were held in a section of the canal that formed a pond. Sometimes, holes were cut in the ice to perform these baptisms. The first church had a tall and slim spire that was referred to as the "darning needle spire." The entire building was remodeled in 1899, and the spire was taken down and was replaced by a tower. (Courtesy of the Rockingham Free Public Library.)

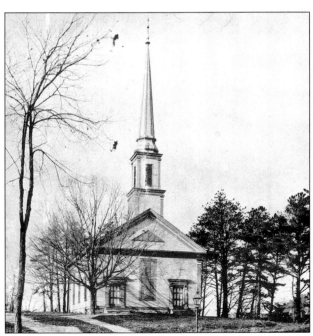

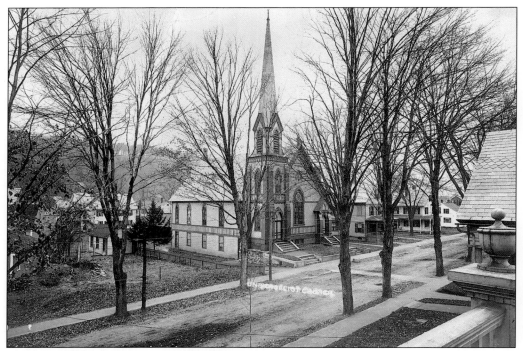

The Universalist church was built in 1880 on a lot purchased from Col. Asa Wentworth on Green Street. The building was razed in 1963, and the land was purchased by Cota & Cota, who operate there today. (Courtesy of the Rockingham Free Public Library.)

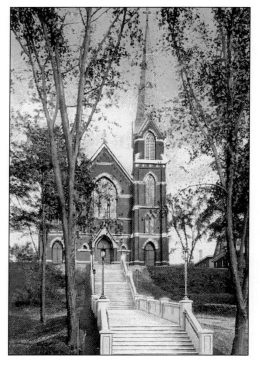

As far as it can be ascertained, the first mass in Rockingham took place in 1848. The St. Charles Catholic Church was erected in 1884. This church is one of two Catholic churches in Bellows Falls. It has a seating capacity of 750. Father Reynolds was responsible for getting the church built, and the cornerstone was laid in June 1884. Father Reynolds also bought a tract of land for a cemetery, located on the Old Terrace in Bellows Falls, in 1894. (Author's collection.)

The Sacred Heart Church was built in 1910. It was the second Catholic church that was built in Bellows Falls. (Courtesy of the Rockingham Free Public Library.)

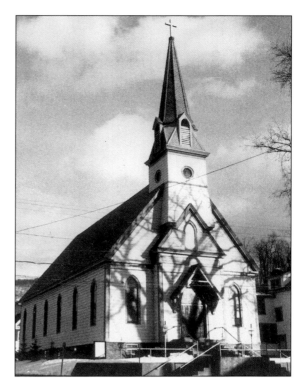

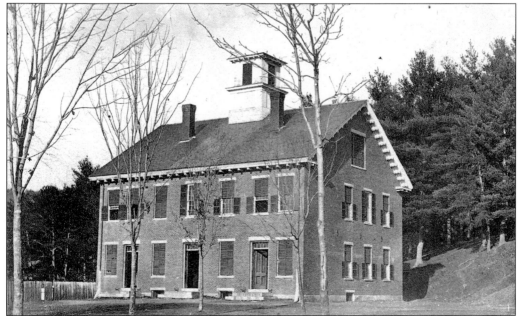

The first high school building was located on Cherry Street. It was built in 1854 and burned in 1866. The loss was an estimated $10,000, and insurance covered between $4,000 and $5,000. At that time, it was the only school in Bellows Falls. (Courtesy of the Rockingham Free Public Library.)

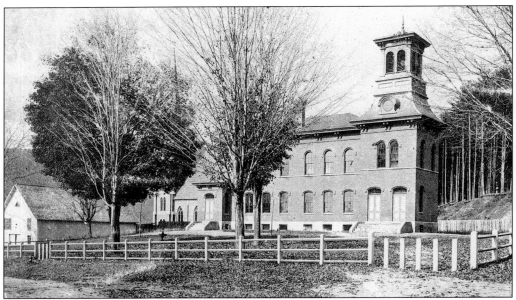

Seen here is the second high school, which was built in 1867. It replaced the first building. Additions were made to the school building in 1887. The building was used as a high school until 1896 and was later sold to the St. Charles Catholic Church, where it served as a parochial school. (Courtesy of the Rockingham Free Public Library.)

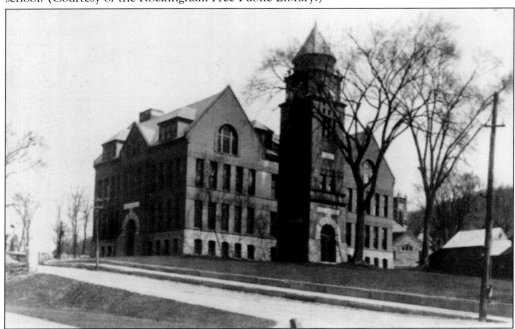

This high school was built in 1896 at a cost of $60,000. It was built with enough rooms to accommodate for the increasing needs for years to come. In addition to the regular school building, the vestries of the Congregational and Baptist churches had been used at various times by the public schools. This school burned in 1925, and another one was built shortly after. (Author's collection.)

This school, built in 1926, replaced the prior school, which burned in 1925. It was a high school until the Bellows Falls Union High School was built. Today, the building serves as the junior high school. (Courtesy of the Rockingham Free Public Library)

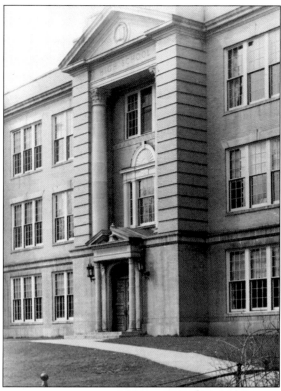

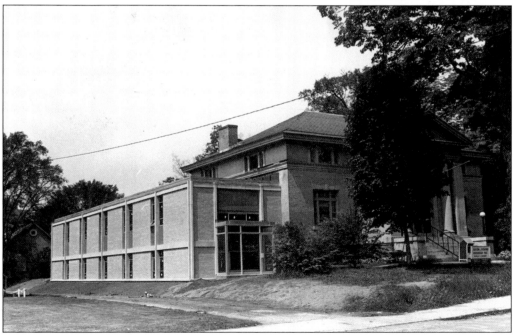

The laying of the cornerstone for the library took place in October 1908. The library was a gift from Andrew Carnegie. (Author's collection.)

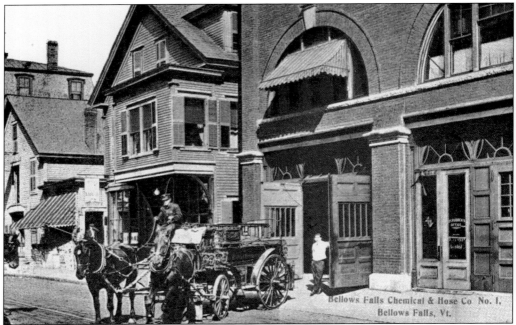

The fire station was first located on Oak Street. It then moved to Rockingham Street, in the square, next to where Oona's Restaurant is. The present fire department is also on Rockingham Street and shares the same building as the police department. (Author's collection.)

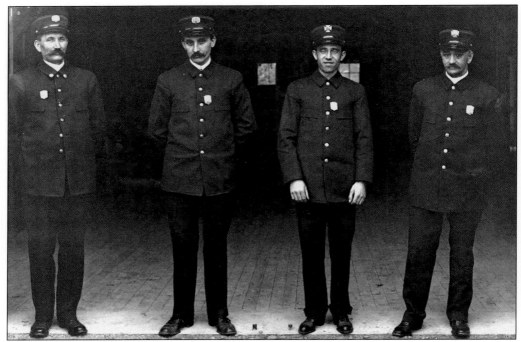

Seen here are four members of the Bellows Falls Fire Department. (Courtesy of the Rockingham Free Public Library.)

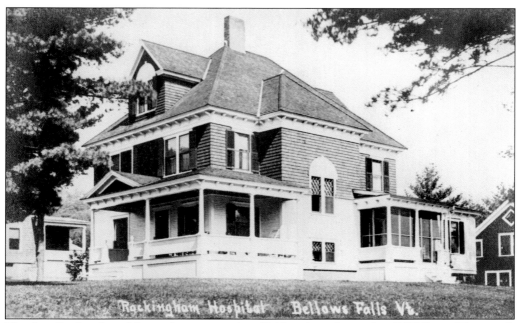

The first Rockingham Hospital was opened in 1912 and was located at 5 Williams Terrace. It had 14 beds. It became too small to accommodate the community's needs. (Courtesy of the Rockingham Free Public Library.)

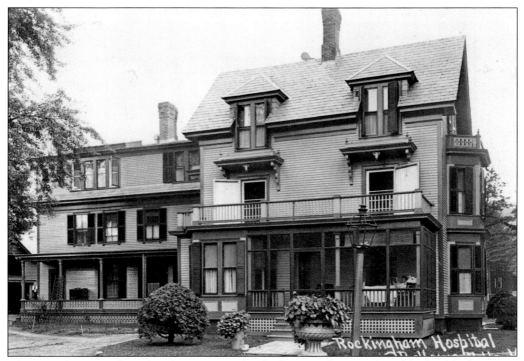

This was the second Rockingham Hospital, which opened in 1915 and had 25 beds. It was located at 50 Pine Street. (Courtesy of the Rockingham Free Public Library.)

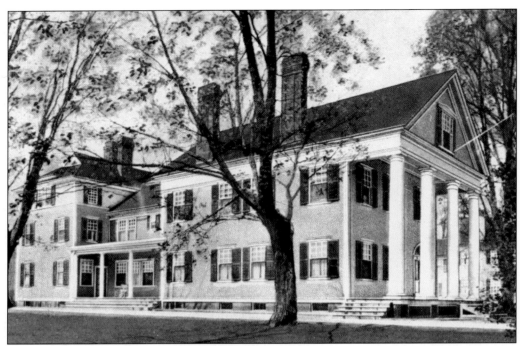

The third Rockingham Hospital was the former home of Mrs. John Wyman Flint and was opened in 1921. A private room at this hospital cost $35 a week. (Courtesy of the Rockingham Free Public Library.)

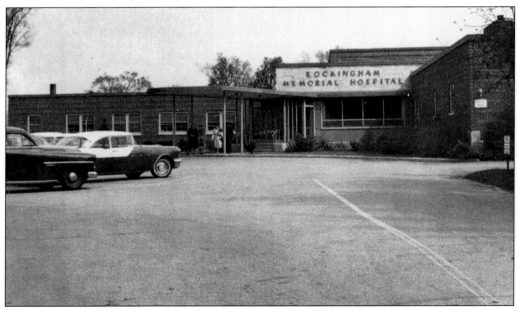

In 1951, Sylvia Green Wilkes, daughter of Hetty Green, gave a $1 million gift for the creation of a new hospital. (Author's collection.)

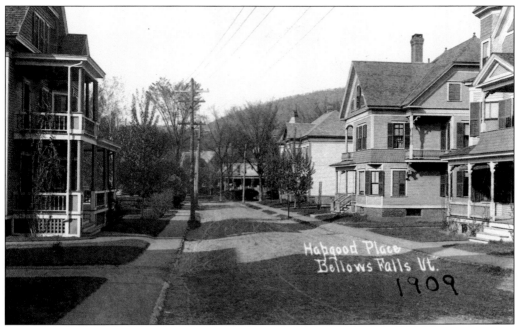

Hapgood Place was named for Solomon Hapgood, whose farmhouse was on the corner of Hapgood and Westminster Streets. The farm was made up of what is now the south part of town. (Courtesy of the Rockingham Free Public Library.)

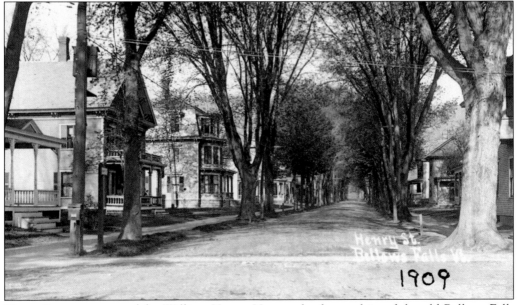

Henry Street was named for William Henry. He was the first cashier of the old Bellows Falls Bank and was later a member of Congress. When the street was laid out, Henry promised that he would set out rows of maples and elms on each side if the street was given his name. He fulfilled his promise. (Courtesy of the Rockingham Free Public Library.)

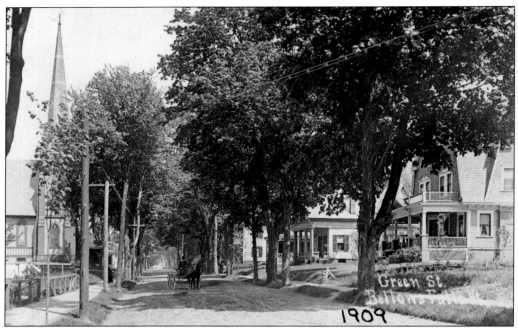

Green Street was named for Francis Green and Henry Atkinson Green, who were prominent men in the community. Through land owned by Henry, the street was laid out. (Courtesy of the Rockingham Free Public Library.)

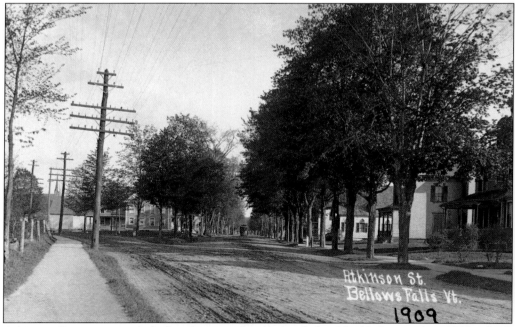

Atkinson Street was named after the same family that helped build the canal in 1792, which they owned for 74 years. (Courtesy of the Rockingham Free Public Library.)

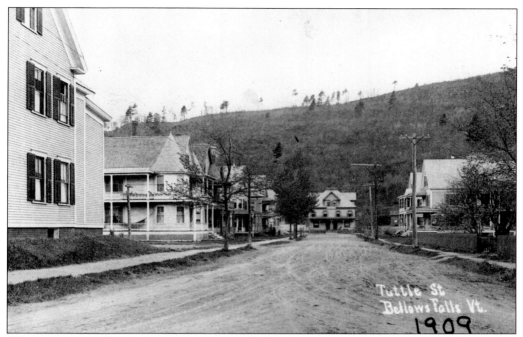

This view shows Tuttle Street. Tuttle was the family name of Lorana Morgan, who was the widow of Quartus Morgan. Quartus had bought the land in 1814. Lorana lived on the farm until her death, and her heirs laid out the streets. (Courtesy of the Rockingham Free Public Library.)

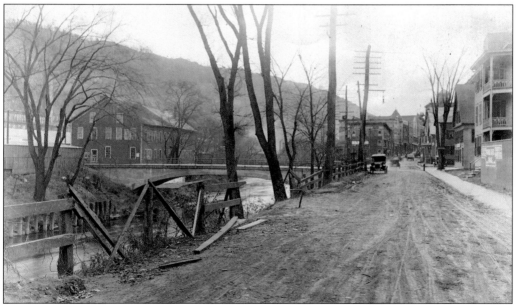

Shown in this early-1900s view is Canal Street, which is a one-way street running from the square to the train depot and canal. The canal operator's houses were also located on this street, and the houses still exist. This road is now tarred, and there is a fence by the canal. (Courtesy of the Rockingham Free Public Library.)

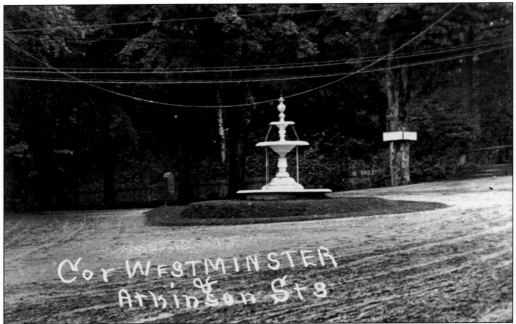

This is the corner of Westminster and Atkinson Streets when the fountain was located on the small common. The fountain was removed and replaced by a garden circle. The war memorial was placed there in 1928. (Courtesy of the Rockingham Free Public Library.)

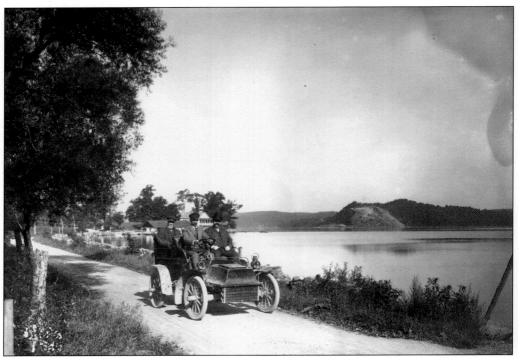

This view shows Route 5, near Roundy's Cove and the boat landing. (Courtesy of Ed Underhill.)

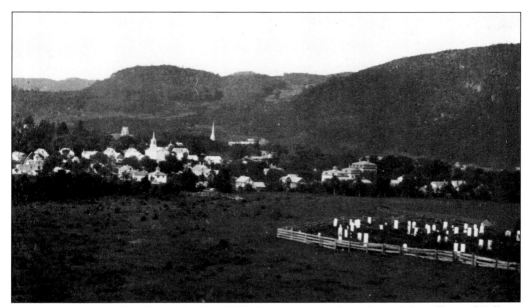

In this photograph, the edge of the Oak Hill Cemetery is on the right and the village of Bellows Falls on the left. Until Oak Hill Cemetery was established, the only graveyards were the Immanuel Church yard and the Catholic cemetery. In 1875, part of the land for the cemetery was bought from the town. In 1883, the balance of 20 acres was bought. J.C. Day was in charge of caretaking. (Courtesy of the Rockingham Free Public Library.)

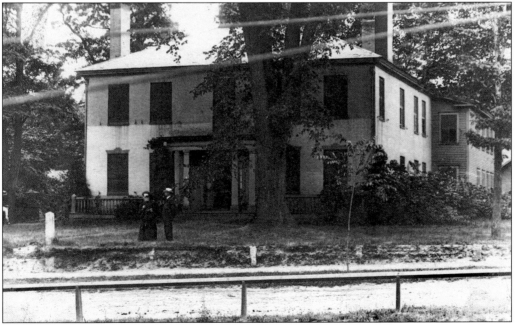

Hetty Green, known as the Witch of Wall Street, is shown outside her home on Church Street with O.M. George. Although she was wealthy, she appeared poor. When her son broke his leg, Hetty would not pay for a doctor, and her son walked with a limp for the rest of his life. (Courtesy of the Rockingham Free Public Library.)

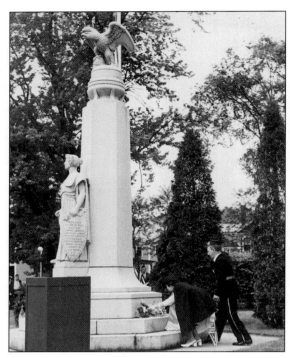

The war memorial replaced the fountain on the island at the foot of "Red Light Hill" in 1928. It was dedicated to the men and women who have served. The memorial is now located in the Hetty Green Park. (Courtesy of the Rockingham Free Public Library.)

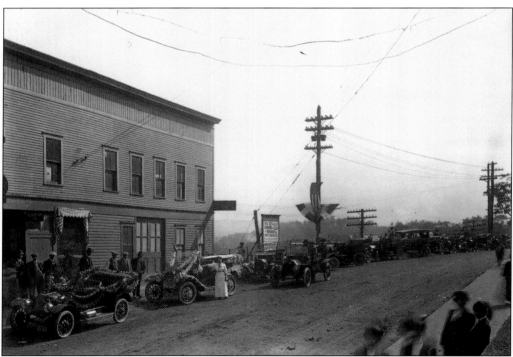

Automobiles line up for a 1913 parade in front of Gates Garage. The building is now empty, but it was once home to a store called Meatland and also a nightclub by the same name. (Courtesy of Ed Underhill.)

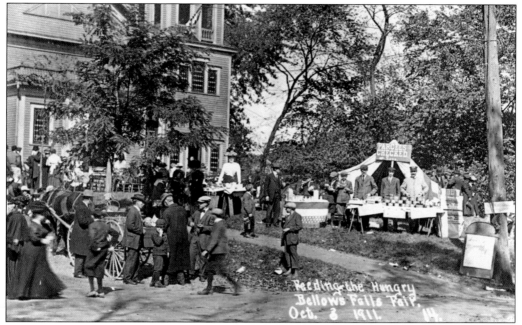

Part of the Bellows Falls Fair is shown in this October 1911 photograph labeled "Feeding the Hungry." This event took place on the lawn of the Baptist church. (Courtesy of the Rockingham Free Public Library.)

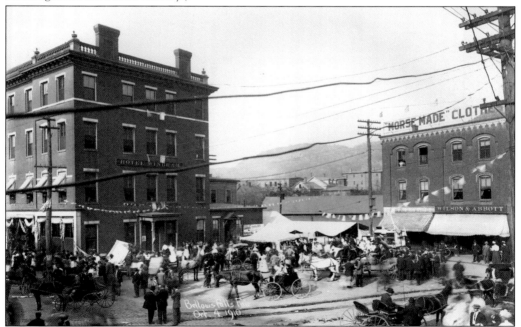

A crowd in the square awaits a parade in October 1910. The building to the right, Wilson & Abbott, was known earlier as the Gray Block, one of the oldest stores in Bellows Falls. It was also known as Howard, Gray, and Taft, and finally as the Star Hotel, which burned. (Courtesy of Ed Underhill.)

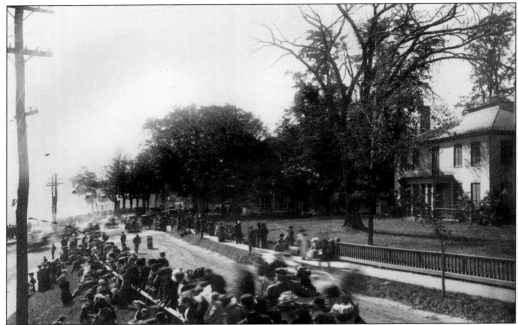

A crowd is watching a parade from Church Place. Hetty Green's house is on the right. It was torn down in 1941. A bank, a parking lot, and the Hetty Green Park are now located there. (Courtesy of Ed Underhill.)

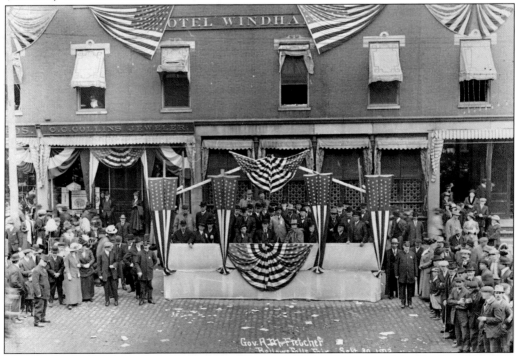

Governor Fletcher reviews a parade in the square in 1913. (Courtesy of the Rockingham Free Public Library.)

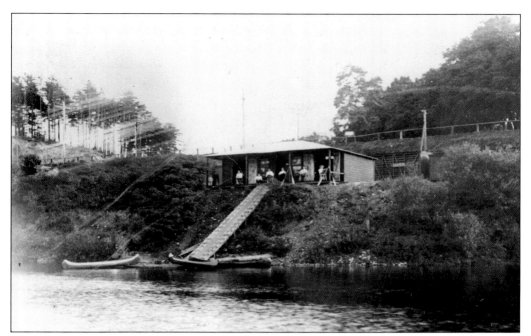

The first clubhouse of the Bellows Falls Boat Club was located north of the Arch Bridge. Originally, it was known as the Bellows Falls Canoe Club. This building was replaced by another building in 1917. (Courtesy of the Rockingham Free Public Library.)

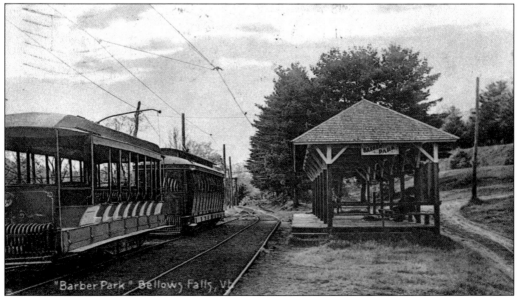

Barber Park was built on land that C.L. Barber, a resident of Bellows Falls, gave to the charter of the Bellows Falls & Saxtons River Street Railway. In the early 1900s, the company was building a road between Bellows Falls and Saxtons River. The park was built midway between Bellows Falls and Saxtons River. The only restrictions were that no liquor could be served in the park and that if it were abandoned by the road, the park would revert back to its heirs. (Author's collection.)

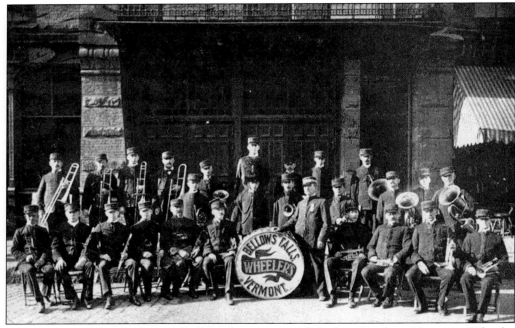

Wheeler's Band, led by George B. Wheeler, was one of the best bands in Vermont. Wheeler led the band for 60 years. The bandleader had requested that his band play during his funeral procession. When he died in 1930, he was accompanied by the band on the long march to the cemetery. (Author's collection.)

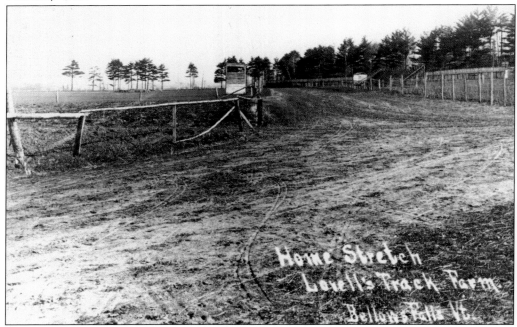

Lovell's Park held races on July 4, 1905. After the races, the farm became known as Lovell's Track Farm. Lewis Lovell bred horses on the farm until the 1920s. The judges' stand was in the center of the field. (Courtesy of the Rockingham Free Public Library.)

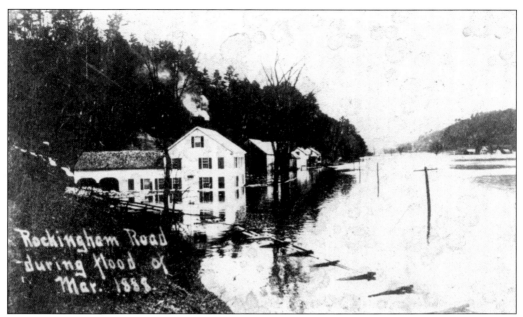

Seen here is a flood in March 1888, which probably was caused by the large amounts of snow that year, namely the snowstorm of March 12. (Courtesy of Ed Underhill.)

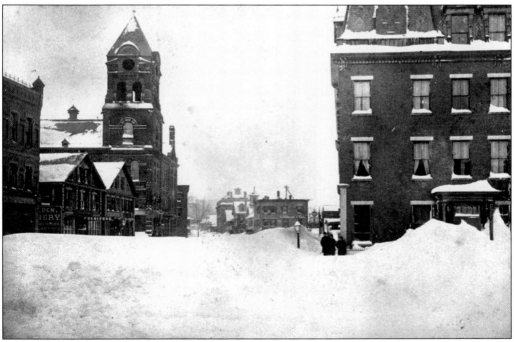

The great blizzard of March 12, 1888, started in the morning and was not considered serious until a gale came in the afternoon and, at times, had the strength of a tornado. The snow continued through the night, and by the next day, snow drifts measured from 20 to 30 feet in depth. The snowfall was measured at 29 inches. (Courtesy of the Rockingham Free Public Library.)

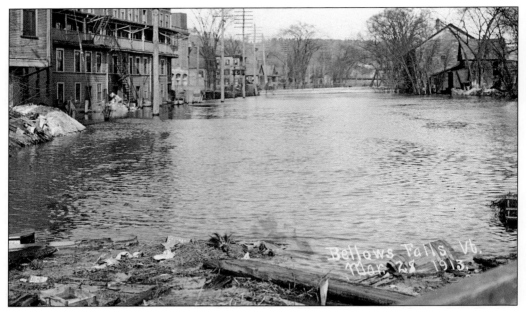

The flood of 1913 was caused by a week of solid rain and melting snow. As logs came hurtling down the river, dynamite was used to divert them from the three railroad bridges. The tunnel under the square was sandbagged when the International Paper mills were flooded under six feet of water. At the depot, baggage and sacks of mail could not be moved due to the platforms being flooded. Travelers were marooned. (Author's collection.)

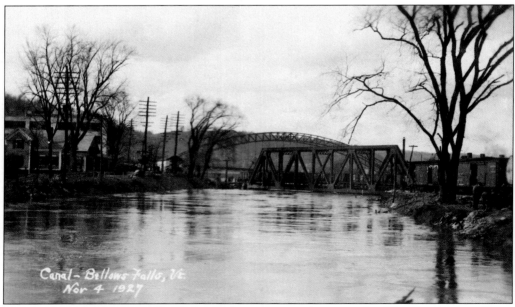

The flood of 1927 was considered the area's worst natural catastrophe. The Connecticut River rose at the rate of a foot an hour, beginning at 4:30 p.m. on the first day. The water rose continually the following day until, at 5:50 p.m., it stood more than 25 feet above the level of the old dam. The depot was four feet deep in water. (Courtesy of Anne Collins)

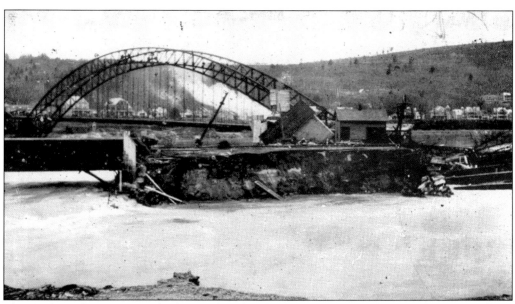

The Arch Bridge was severely damaged in the flood of 1938. This photograph shows Bellows Falls in the background. (Author's collection.)

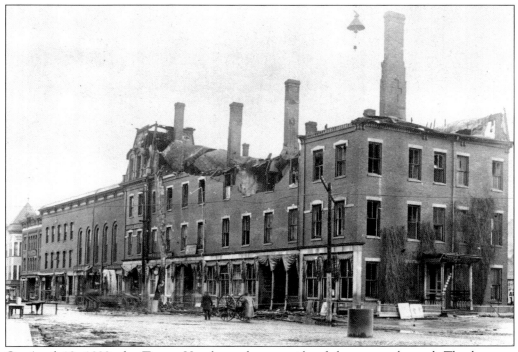

On April 12, 1899, the Towns Hotel, on the east side of the square, burned. The loss was estimated at $20,000. It was rebuilt and named the Hotel Windham. (Courtesy of the Rockingham Free Public Library.)

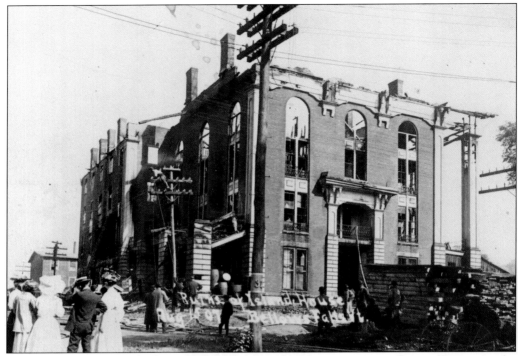

The Island House was built in 1850 as a resort for summer visitors. Originally, it was the home of Dr. Samuel Cutler in 1792. In 1850, it was remodeled into a hotel by Col. Roswell Shurtleff. It burned twice, the first time in 1907. It burned completely in 1965. (Courtesy of the Rockingham Free Public Library.)

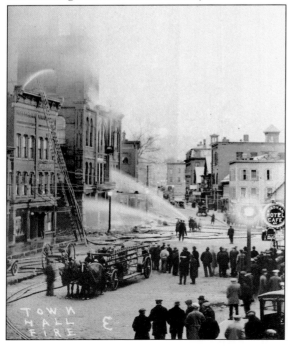

The town hall and opera house building burned on May 10, 1925. It had been built in 1887. The building housed the post office, library, the store of F.G. Pierce, and a banquet hall. It was the town's largest building. (Author's collection.)

This is the town hall after the fire. There was much ruin, and it was a great loss for the town. (Author's collection.)

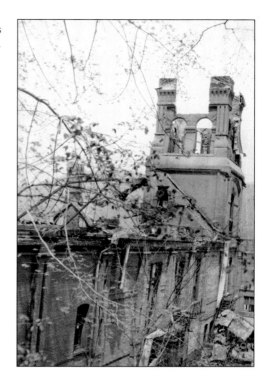

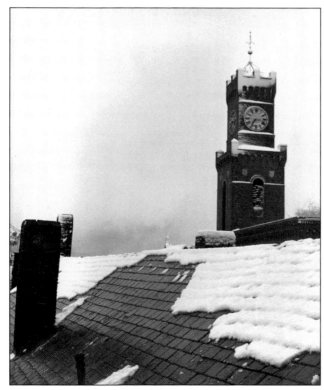

This new town hall replaced the one that burned in 1925. It has a movie theater, and the town offices are located here. This photograph was taken by Ed Underhill, who stood on a roof to get the picture. (Courtesy of Ed Underhill.)

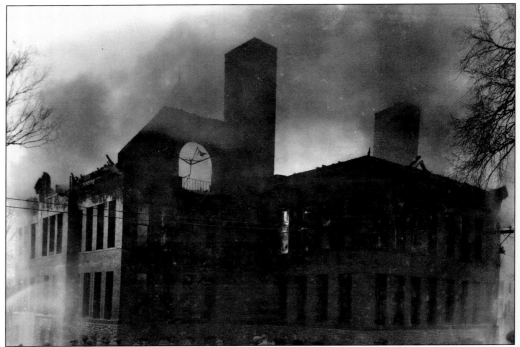

The high school burned on November 26, 1925. The fire began at 6:30 a.m. It burned so quickly that the building was gone by 9:00 a.m. It was fortunate that school was not in session at the time. (Courtesy of Ed Underhill.)

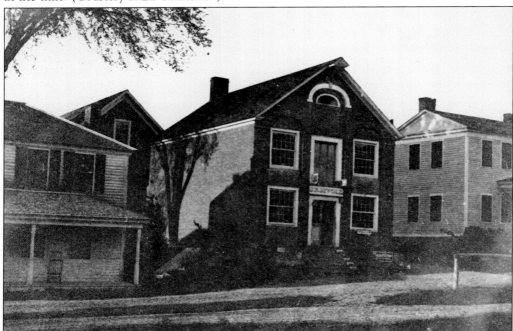

This brick building was the post office and was also Josiah Divoll's store. This building burned in 1909, along with other buildings. (Courtesy of the Rockingham Free Public Library.)

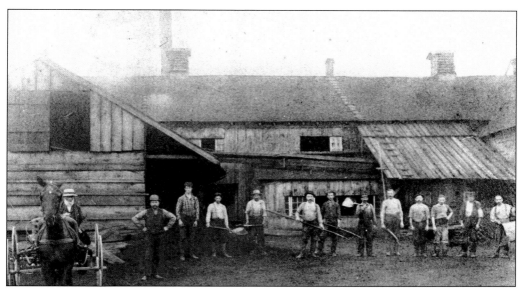

Mannasseh Divoll, a tanner and currier, came to Rockingham village c. 1806. He set up a tannery in Rockingham and became a prominent citizen despite the fact that he had been "warned out" in 1807. "Warning out" meant that the town would serve notice on people in their first year of residency; if their business failed, they would be prevented from gaining residence so that the town would not have to support them. Holding office automatically relieved the disability caused by the "warning out" process. (Courtesy of the Rockingham Free Public Library.)

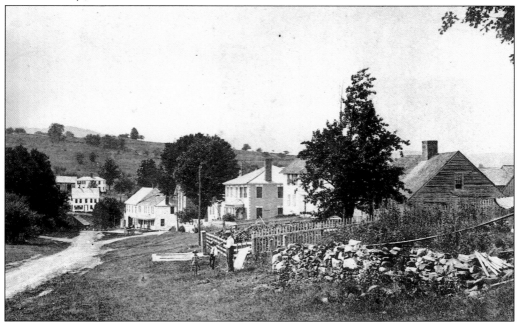

Rockingham village, known as Old Town, burned in April 1909. The post office, a store, and several other buildings were destroyed in about three hours. (Courtesy of the Rockingham Free Public Library.)

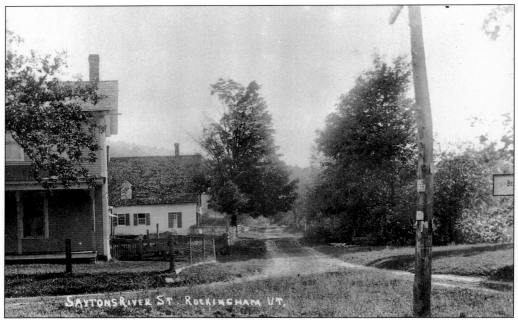

This was one of the streets in Rockingham that burned in 1909. Although the village was never rebuilt after the fire, many residents still live there. (Courtesy of the Rockingham Free Public Library.)

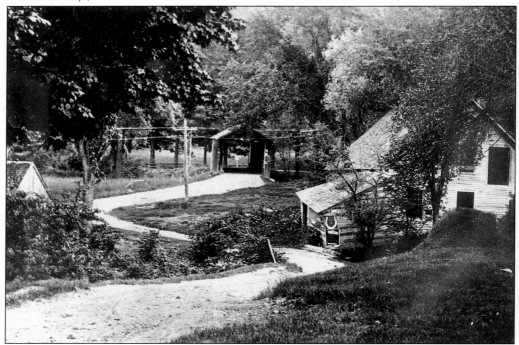

Cambridgeport is located several miles up the river from Saxtons River. It had woolen mills, a gristmill, and a soapstone shop. There was a store, church, schoolhouse, and many nice residences. (Courtesy of the Rockingham Free Public Library.)

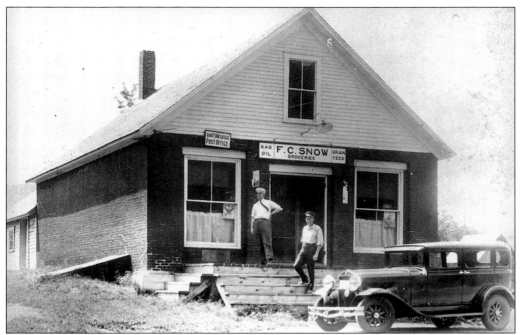

In 1869, Bartonsville had two blacksmith shops, two sawmills, a carriage shop, and a new depot. It was a busy town with a paper mill that employed about 50 people. The paper business went to Bellows Falls when the railroad track was built. Seen in this photograph is Snow's country store, which was also a post office. (Courtesy of the Rockingham Free Public Library.)

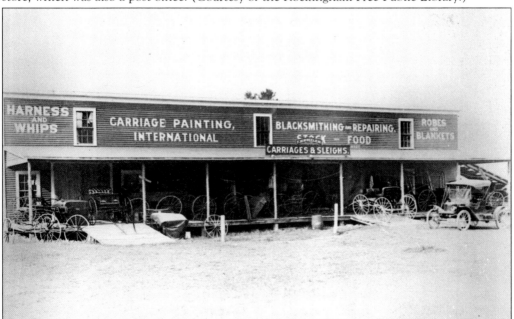

Wheeler's Carriage House stood near the junction of a street in Rockingham and Route 103. Wheeler painted and sold carriages and sleighs. He later dealt in automobiles. (Courtesy of the Rockingham Free Public Library.)

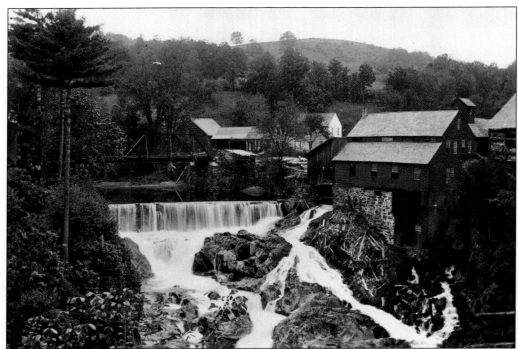

Lawrence Mills was owned and operated by Martin R. Lawrence, who came from Windsor. The original name of the company was Nourse & Cogswell, and at that time, there was only a board, saw, and flouring mill. Lawrence expanded the business to make wooden wares. He employed anywhere from five to a dozen men. It is now called Brockaway Mills. (Courtesy of the Rockingham Free Public Library.)

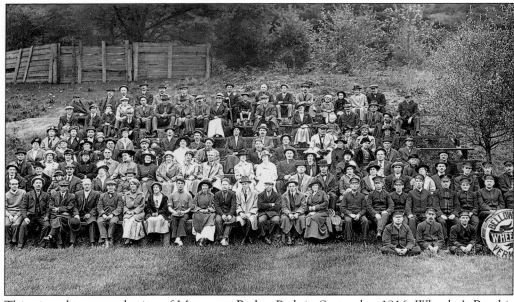

This view shows a gathering of Masons at Barber Park in September 1916. Wheeler's Band is seated to the right. (Author's collection.)

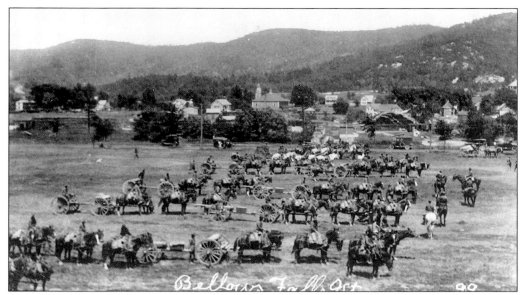

The original owner of Morgan's Field was Quartus Morgan, who had a large farm on the land. He subdivided it in 1895 into building lots. This photograph shows how Morgan's Field was used for military purposes. Teddy Roosevelt spoke at Morgan's Field in 1902, when he was running for president. In its history, this plot of land has been used for many things, including the circus, gardens, and an ice-skating rink. It is now a residential section. (Author's collection.)

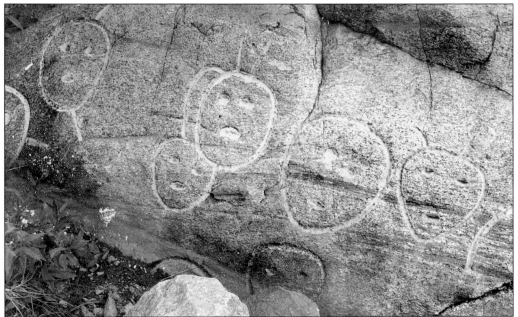

These Native American petroglyphs are located under the Vilas Bridge. It is estimated that they are 300 to 2,000 years old. They are the area's most pronounced and interesting memento of the Native Americans. It is thought that the carvings commemorate an event in which a chief and members of his tribe performed some noted exploit or met with some disaster. (Courtesy of Ed Underhill.)

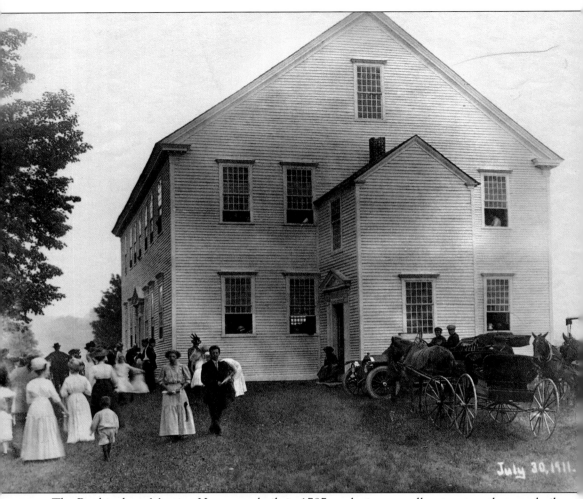

The Rockingham Meeting House was built in 1787, replacing a smaller structure that was built in 1744. This building was used for worship for 42 years, and town meetings were also held there until 1869. Inside, there is a gallery on three sides. There are square pews, and the pulpit was built high. It was restored to its original condition in 1906. On May 16, 2000, the building was designated a National Historic Site. (Courtesy of the Rockingham Free Public Library.)

Two

WESTMINSTER

Westminster is one of Vermont's oldest and most historic towns, beginning as Township No. 1, or New Taunton, under the jurisdiction of the Massachusetts Bay Colony in 1734. There was no permanent settlement until 1751, when a new survey of Massachusetts placed No. 1, with the name of Westminster, in the New Hampshire Grants. In 1762, King George III decreed that the Connecticut River was the boundary between New Hampshire and New York. Westminster became a part of Cumberland County, New York, and became the county seat in 1772.

It was time for the March 1775 court session to consider action to collect debts. This court was run by Tory judges. The Loyalist domination proved to be too much for area colonists. Several men tried, without success, to dissuade the judge from holding court. When the "Yorkers" still insisted on holding court, people here rebelled.

A group of citizens, armed only with clubs from a neighbor's woodpile, entered the courthouse on the afternoon of March 13, 1775. While the patriots were in possession of the building, they were attacked by the Tories, resulting in the death of two patriots and injury to others.

About 500 patriots equipped for war, including members of Ethan Allen's Green Mountain Boys, quickly assembled in Westminster the next day. On a decision made by a committee formed by the patriots, the judge and other court officials were taken to prison in Northampton, Massachusetts. Cumberland County Court sessions were never again held in this county under the rule of Great Britain's King George. This event, known as the Westminster Massacre, occurring one month before the Battle of Lexington, was considered by some to have been the first blood shed in the Revolutionary War. The Cumberland County Court was located in Westminster from 1772 to 1775. Later, the building was the scene of many historic meetings and conventions. Perhaps the most unusual was in January 1777, when citizens declared Vermont to be a free and independent republic, which lasted until Vermont joined the United States in 1791 as the 14th state.

The old court building stood unoccupied from 1787, when Newfane became the county seat, until 1806, when it was sold and torn down.

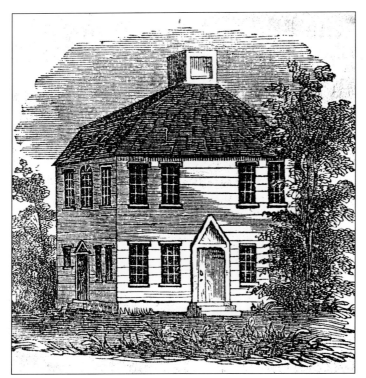

The Westminster Court House, built in 1772, was the scene of the Westminster Massacre. The conflict took place on March 13, 1775. The building was torn down by Isaiah Eaton c. 1806. A monument erected in 1902 now marks its location at the top of Courthouse Hill, King's Highway (Route 5). A model of this building is on display at the Westminster Historical Society museum.

Seen here is the tombstone of William French, who was the first man killed in the Westminster Massacre. He was only 22 at the time of his death. This gravestone was replaced by a much more impressive monument to French, which can be found in Westminster's Old East Parish Cemetery, on King's Highway.

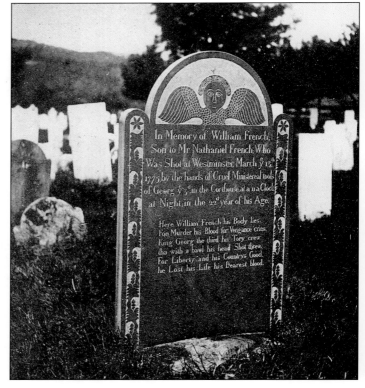

The Old Westminster Meeting House, which was constructed in 1770, stood in the center of King's Highway. The main street in Westminster Village was laid out during the reign of King George II as a training ground and called King's Highway. This large building was later moved back so that the façade lined up with neighboring houses. It was destroyed by fire in 1888 after a lightning strike. This building was replaced by the present town hall.

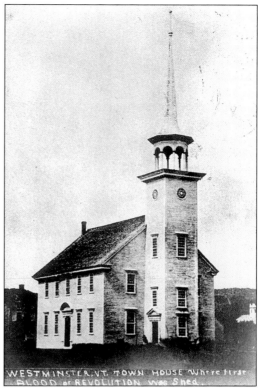

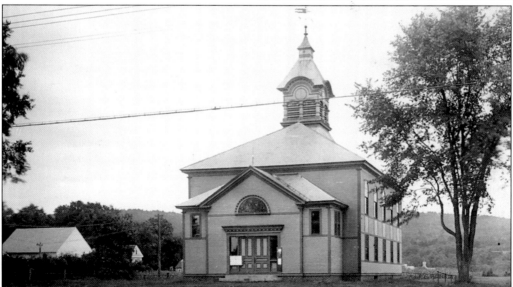

Built on the site of the Old Westminster Meeting House in 1889, the present-day town hall has been repeatedly struck by lightning but has not suffered the same fate as its predecessor. The meeting room on the second floor accommodated town meetings, theatrical productions, and various other entertainment for town residents. This second floor currently houses the Westminster Historical Society's museum.

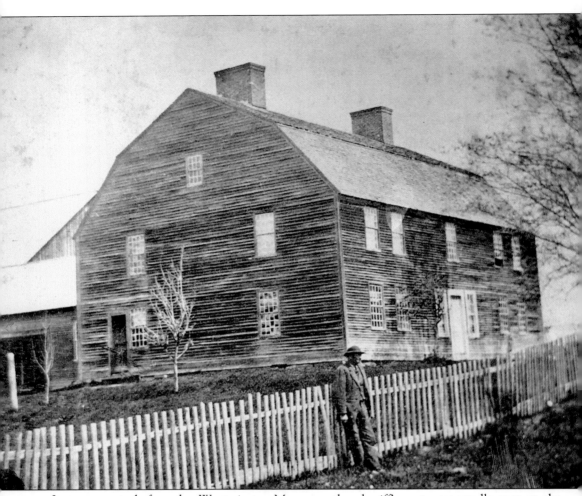

Just moments before the Westminster Massacre, the sheriff's party reportedly met at the Norton Tavern. The patriots had taken possession of the courthouse to prevent the New York court from sitting. The Cumberland County, New York sheriff and his men led the charge up Courthouse Hill to regain control. Later referred to as the Tory Tavern, the tavern stood on Westminster Flats, in Westminster Village. This building was torn down in the last quarter of the 19th century.

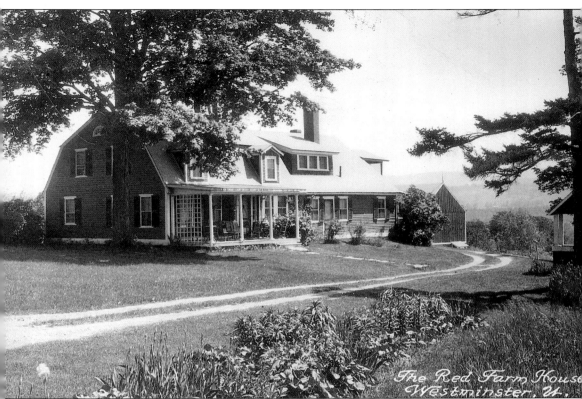

This red farmhouse, originally the Gilson Tavern, was one of Westminster's early taverns. Built c. 1760, it still stands a few miles south of the village. With the distinctive gambrel roof, it is an excellent example of 18th-century architecture.

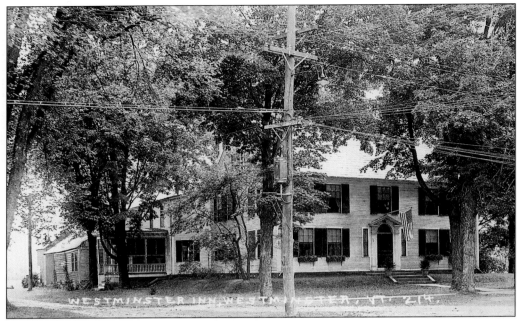

Located on King's Highway, the Mark Richards House served as the Westminster Inn in the first half of the 20th century. This elegant establishment was lost to fire on New Year's Day in 1947. Mark Richards, a prominent citizen, local merchant, and Vermont legislator for many years, served in Congress from 1817 to 1820.

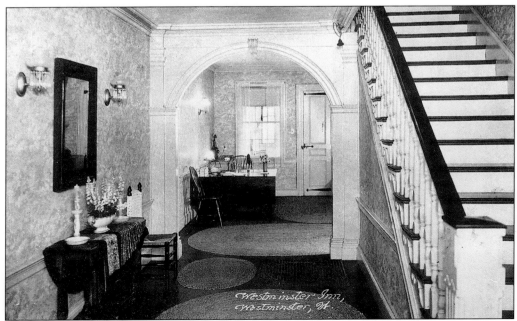

This view of the interior of the Westminster Inn shows its welcoming front hall.

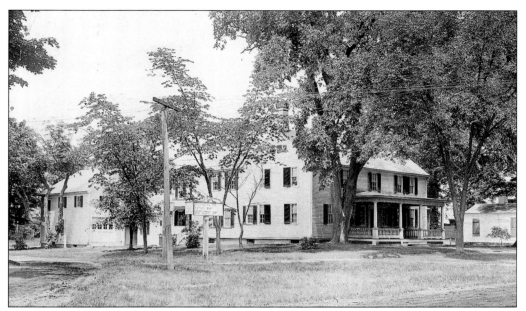

The William Czar Bradley House was the home of Westminster's most illustrious citizen. Born in 1782, Bradley attended Yale University at age 13 and was admitted to the bar at age 20. At 24, Bradley was a town representative. He was elected to Congress in 1813 at age 31. Bradley died in Westminster in 1867. This beautiful home, reported to have been a wedding gift from his bride's parents, still stands on King's Highway.

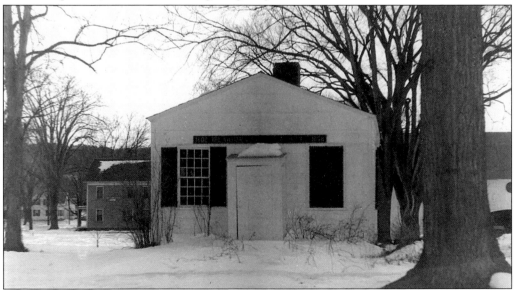

This small building, the law office of William Czar Bradley, was last used in 1860. When it was unlocked in 1998, it was as if time had stood still. Inside was an unbelievable treasure trove of original features: wallpaper, documents, furniture, and artifacts—all just as they might have been left when Bradley locked the door for the last time. Located adjacent to the William Czar Bradley House, this structure is now owned by the Westminster Historical Society and is open to the public on summer Sunday afternoons.

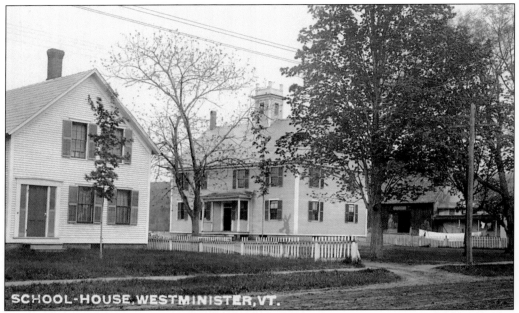

This building on School Street was built in 1850 to house the Westminster Seminary, a private school directed by Prof. Lafayette Ward. It was later used by the town as a grammar school until 1953. This building is now divided into five apartments.

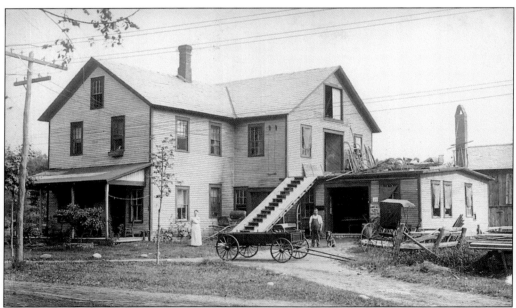

B.F. (Byron F.) Atcherson Carriage and Sleigh Factory, on School Street, stood across from the present Westminster Center School. Note that carriages were produced on the second floor and were rolled down the ramp when completed.

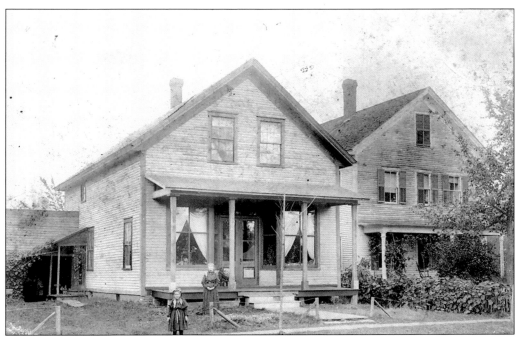

The building on the left, known as the Waldron-Spencer House, was constructed as a store by the owner of the residence on the right. By 1920, the store was converted into a private residence and the home to the right had been purchased by the Boyden Grange No. 157. Both buildings, now privately owned, stand today on School Street.

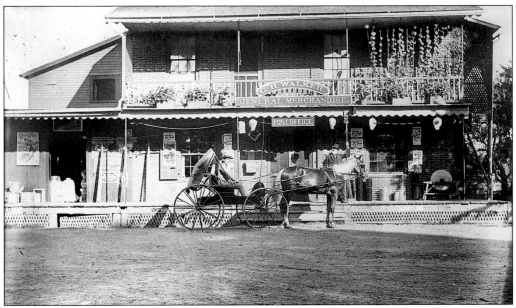

The Walker Store was located on King's Highway in the center of the village. It was housed in a brick building predating 1807, which was destroyed by fire on February 18, 1922. This building originally held Vermont's first state bank, which issued currency bearing the name Westminster.

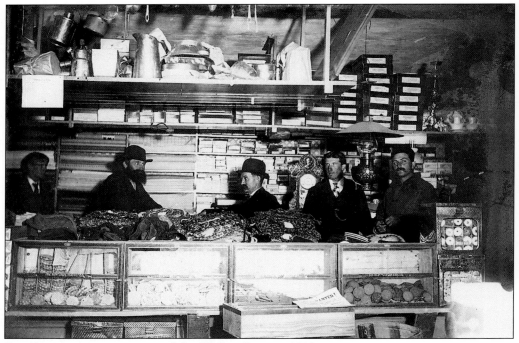
Seen here is an interior view of the Walker Store c. 1900.

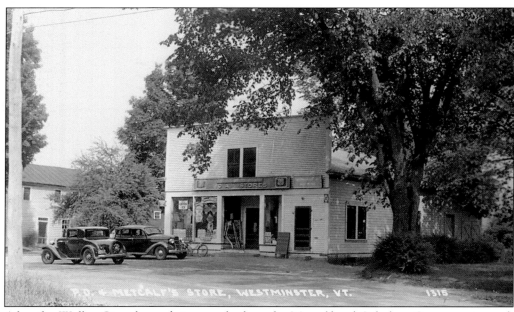
After the Walker Store burned, it was rebuilt as the Metcalf and Cahalane Store, as pictured. The false façade was removed after 1945. This property was home to a series of general stores owned by different proprietors until 2001, when it finally closed its doors.

Located along King's Highway, the Congregational Church of the East Parish is just one story tall in this photograph. The church was built in 1835 after a controversy over the use of the Old Westminster Meeting House.

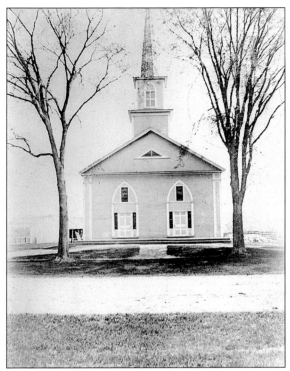

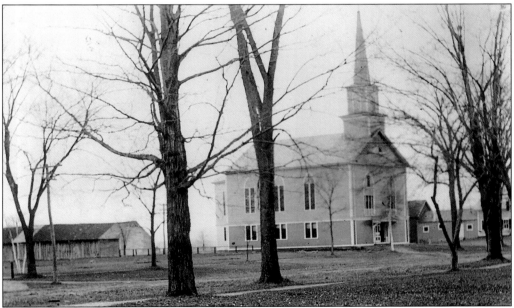

The same church was raised sometime between 1902 and 1903 to its present configuration. This was a common practice as congregations grew and styles changed. Mainly Greek Revival in style, this building has the sanctuary raised to the second floor, with the new first story to provide a vestry and kitchen. The two former entries on the front façade were replaced with stained-glass windows.

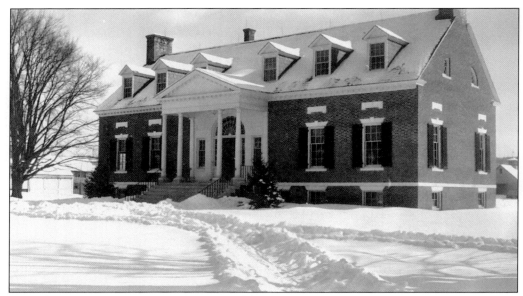

The Westminster Institute and Butterfield Library are situated on King's Highway near the center of the village. George Dascomb and Isaac Butterfield funded the project, giving the Westminster East Parish a community center with a stage, gymnasium, and library. Construction of this impressive Colonial Revival building was begun in 1922, and it was dedicated on July 30, 1924.

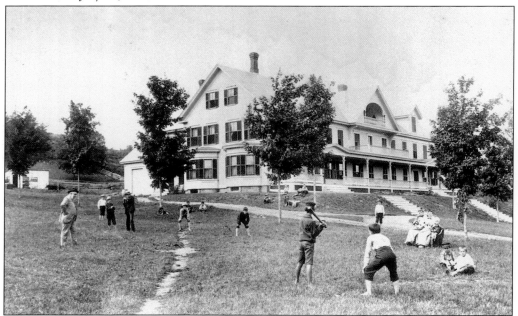

The main building of Kurn Hattin Homes originally served as the school and dormitory for 30 boys, administrative offices, and living quarters for the superintendent, matron, and several staff members until 1908. Rev. Charles Dickinson, a native of Westminster, established Kurn Hattin, a school for homeless and neglected boys. Children learned farm tasks and social skills along with their schooling, as the school's boys and girls do today.

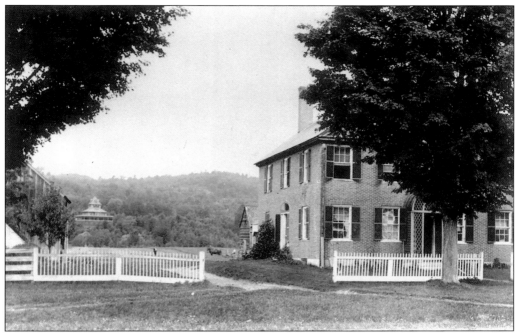

The Dickinson House on King's Highway was built by the father of the founder of Kurn Hattin Homes. Rev. Charles Dickinson lived here as a child. Note the exotic pagoda building in the background in Evan's Woods. F.L. Temple filled the surrounding gardens of this fanciful structure with 7,000 cultivated roses and an equally exotic garden. The pagoda was destroyed by fire.

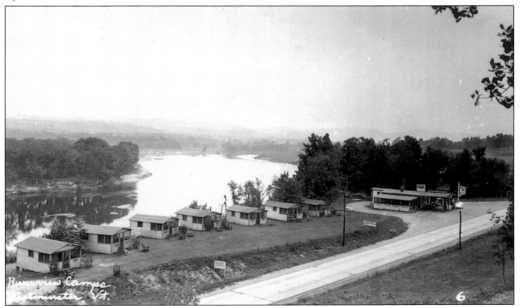

Riverview Camps was one of several roadside campgrounds that were popular before the modern motel and the coming of Interstate 91. With views of the Connecticut River, many such tourist accommodations were located along Route 5.

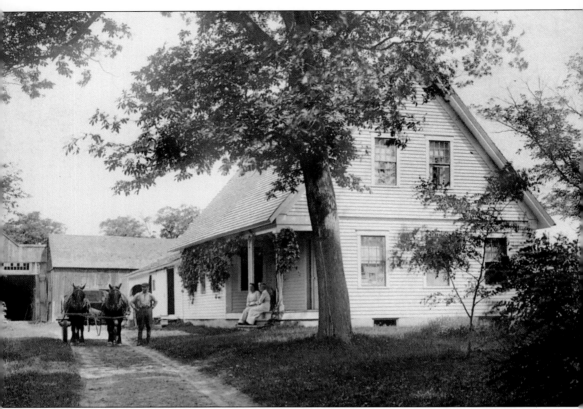

Henry Augustus Willard left this house on Piggery Road to establish the famous Willard Hotel in Washington, D.C. There is a marker on the front lawn that denotes the spot where the Willard family first settled in Westminster in the 1700s. The family returned to Westminster early in the 20th century and purchased the William Czar Bradley House. The Willard family provided the town with the watering trough at the town hall and the wrought-iron fence surrounding the Old East Parish Cemetery.

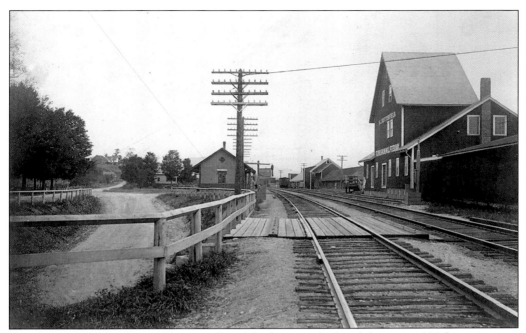

Westminster Station boasted a gristmill and feed store, which celebrates its 100th anniversary in 2002. The railroad depot building, although no longer available for rail passenger service, has served the public as a gas station, antique auction house, and a convenience store.

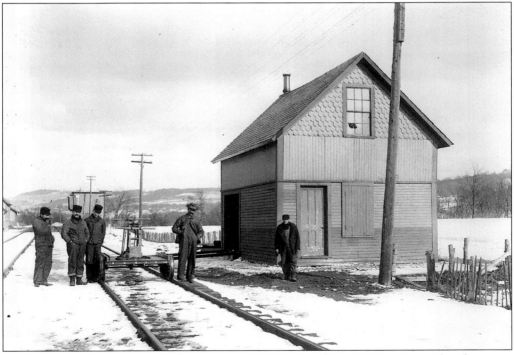

Grout Station, at the east end of Grout Avenue, was one of two Westminster railroad stations and is now a private residence.

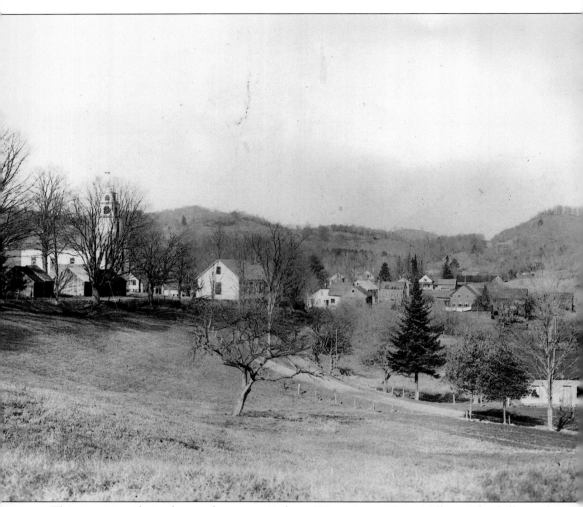

This is a view from the southern approach to Westminster West Village. The hills in the background of the c. 1900 photograph are now completely wooded. Dirt roads like this were fine until mud season!

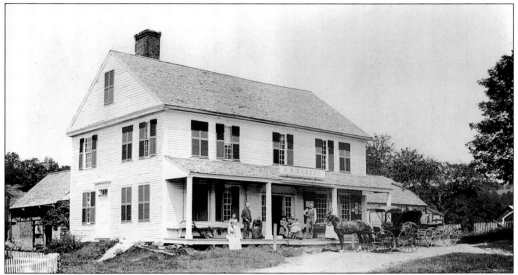

The A.P. Ranney General Store, in Westminster West Village, was erected in 1805 and used as a tavern until 1856, when it became a store. Some of the successive owners were Ephraim Wilcox, 1856; A.P. Ranney, 1872; W.A. Gorham, 1894; and F.R. Chapman, 1899. The building is now a private residence. Seen here are, from left to right, Mary Clark (second wife of A.P. Ranney), unidentified, Henry Hall, unidentified, Hattie Phillips (first wife of A.P. Ranney), A.P. Ranney, and Delia Ranney (later Mrs. Alfred Hall).

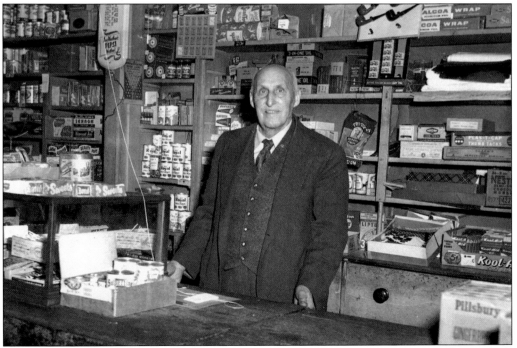

Frank Chapman, proprietor of Chapman's General Store, in Westminster West Village, which was formerly the A.P. Ranney Store, is ready to greet customers. Note the variety of goods available in this small rural store.

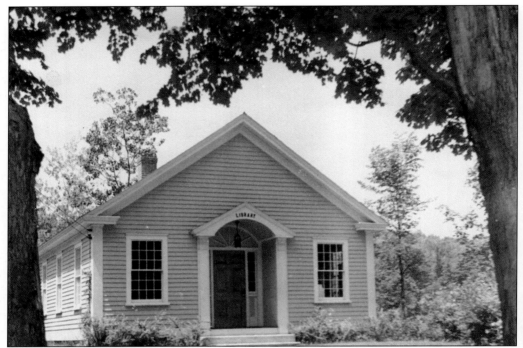

The Westminster West Public Library still serves the community. It was built in 1936 for $1,500 on land donated by Martha Miller. The library association was originally founded in 1870 and was known as the Ladies Aid Society.

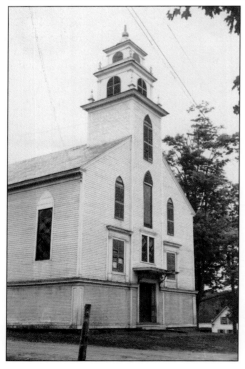

The Congregational Church of Westminster West, originally constructed in 1830, burned in 1988 and has been replaced by a new one of a similar design.

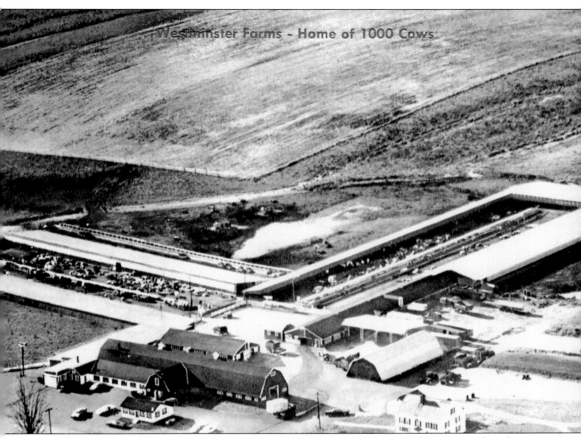

Pictured c. 1960 is "Westminster Farms—Home of 1000 Cows." This was the largest of six farms owned and operated by Bruno and Pauline Bazin. It had previously been the Fenn Farm and is now owned by the Goodells. Dairy farming is still quite active in Westminster.

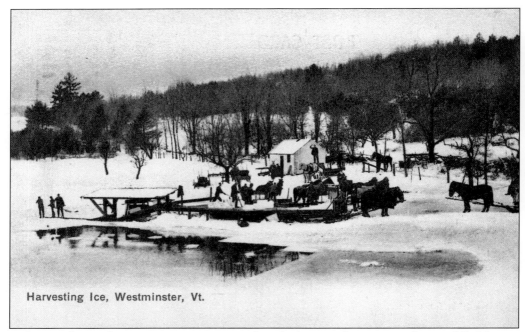

Harvesting Ice, Westminster, Vt.

Before modern refrigeration, ice was cut and packed in sawdust. It was then peddled by ice wagons for use in iceboxes. This pond on Kurn Hattin Road was located below the New East Parish Cemetery. It was known as the Lane and Richardson Pond.

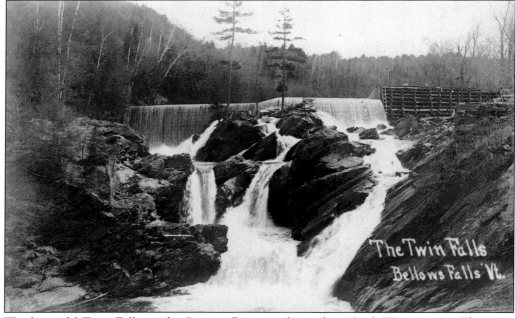

The Twin Falls, Bellows Falls, Vt.

The beautiful Twin Falls on the Saxtons River are located in North Westminster. This river provided waterpower for early industry and manufacturing, which included a woolen mill, paper mill, sawmill, box shop, and an electric power plant.

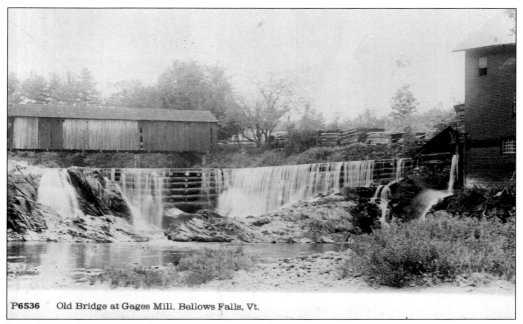

P6536   Old Bridge at Gages Mill, Bellows Falls, Vt.

In 1835, Sanford Granger built this bridge over the Saxtons River in North Westminster using timber from his mill at a cost of $702. It was destroyed by fire in the 1960s; arson was suspected. Granger also built the Tucker Toll Bridge in Bellows Falls.

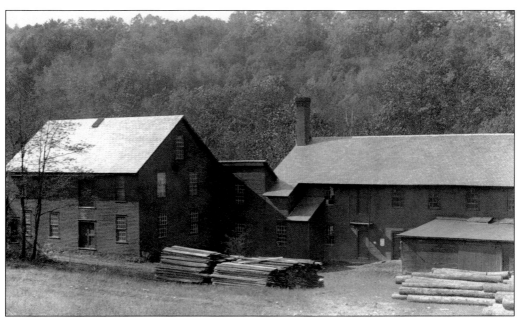

The Gage Basket Factory on the Saxtons River was owned and operated by the Sidney Gage family. It was established in 1842 by brothers William P. and H.F. Gage. This business produced fine baskets into the 20th century. In this photograph, stacks of native oak and ash lumber are ready to be made into splint, which was woven into many different styles of baskets. It was this factory that gave North Westminster the name Gageville.

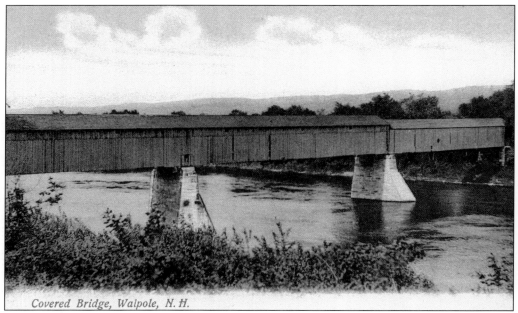

Covered Bridge, Walpole, N.H.

This covered bridge over the Connecticut River linked Vermont to Walpole, New Hampshire, at Westminster Station. The Connecticut River served as a highway for the early settlers. Canoes and flatboats were employed to transport people, livestock, and goods up and down the river.

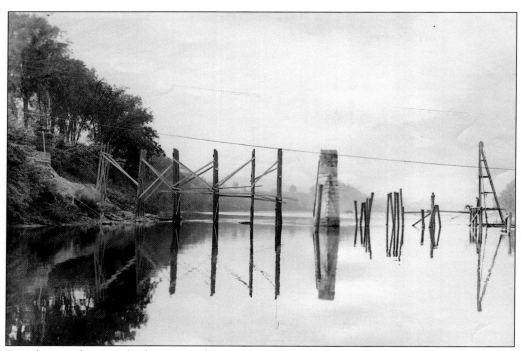

Seen here is the same bridge pictured in 1910, after it was destroyed by fire. Rumor has it that the fire was set by an irate husband to stop his wife from visiting her lover, who lived across the river. She learned to swim.

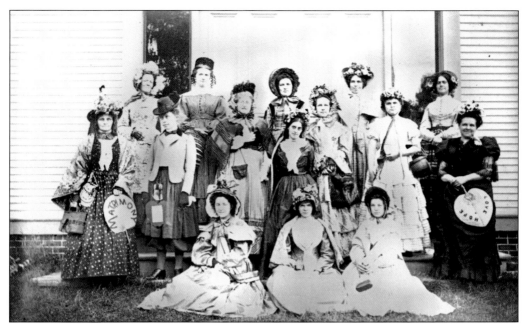

The cast of the production *Old Maids Convention* poses on the steps of the Westminster Town Hall. It was a very popular play c. 1900 and was performed in many towns. Some of the characters portrayed are Calamity Jane Higgins, Tiny Short, Patience Desire Mann, Charity Longface, Hannah Biggerstaff, Frances Touchmenot, and Professor Makeover.

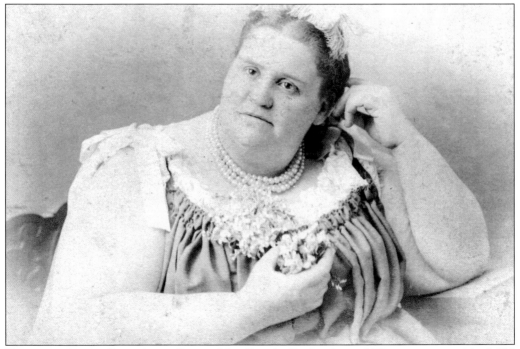

Known professionally as Annie Porter, Mrs. Dwight Fairbrother, of Westminster, weighed 400 pounds and traveled with the Ringling Brothers and Barnum & Bailey Circus.

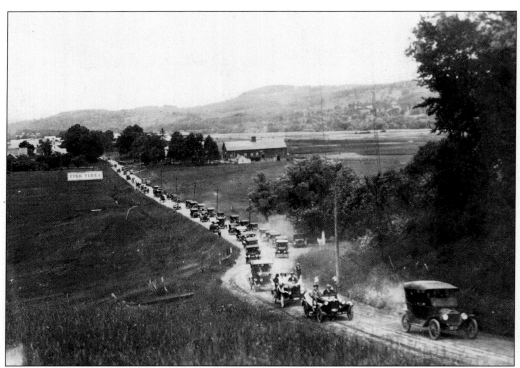

This parade up Courthouse Hill celebrated the end of World War I. The curving approach to King's Highway was straightened when the road was paved.

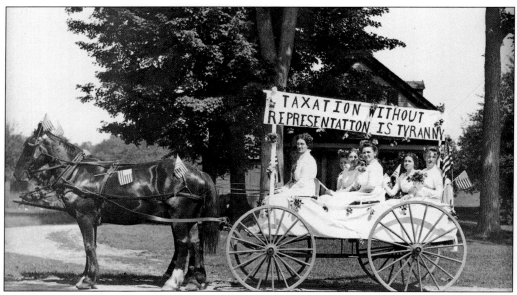

"Taxation without representation is tyranny" was an example of rural patriotism, exhibited in a Fourth of July parade.

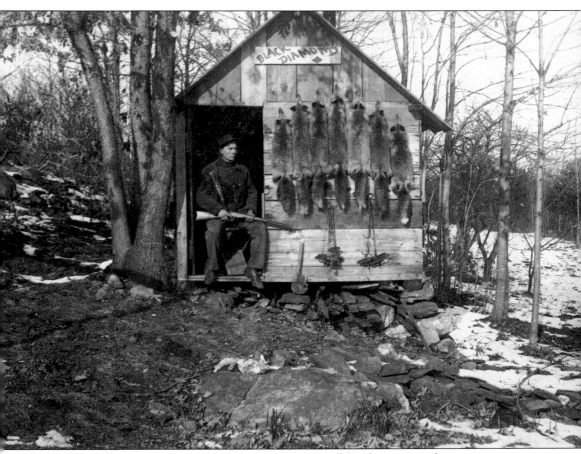

Lynn Fullam, a Westminster resident, proudly shows off his hunting and trapping success c. 1906.

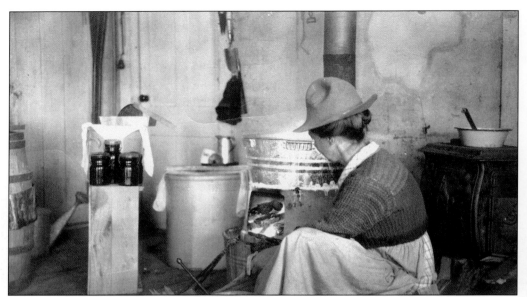

Bertha Miller Collins, wife of the manager of the Connecticut Valley Orchards, preserves the harvest in her summer kitchen c. 1917.

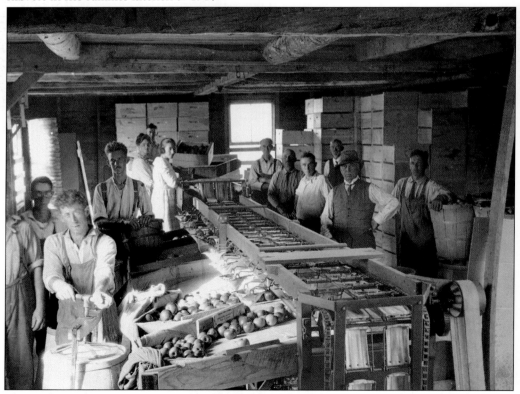

The packing plant at Connecticut Valley Orchards was located in the Rocky Hill section of Westminster. The orchard was begun in 1911. Young men and women picked, packed, and shipped apples to New York City and throughout New England.

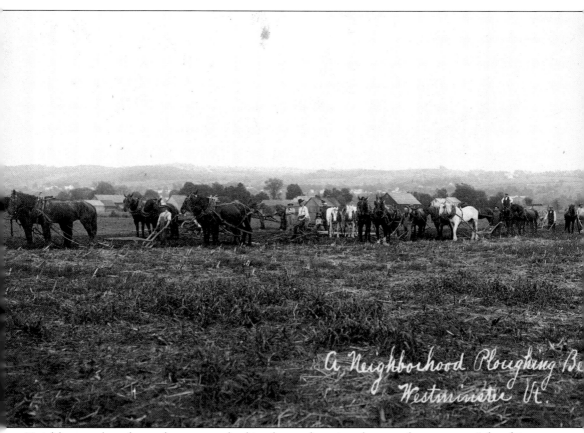

Neighbors gathered together to get the big chores done in what was known as a "ploughing bee." The farmland of the Connecticut River basin is said to be the most fertile for hundreds of miles. Geologists believe this land to be an ancient lake bottom; its rich soil still produces the finest agricultural products.

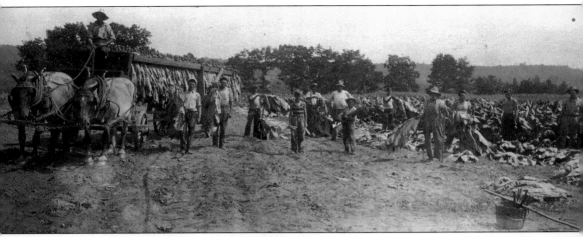

Westminster was famous for growing the select leaves used for cigar wrappers. This c. 1932 view shows the Charles Holton farm.

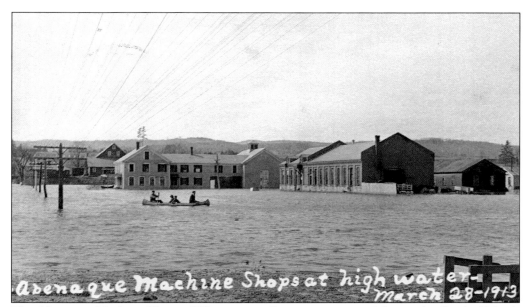

The Abenaque Machine Shops of Westminster Station are pictured during the flood of March 28, 1913. There have been many times that the Connecticut River has overflowed its banks, causing serious problems for low-lying areas of Westminster. The Abenaque engines were produced here from 1890 to 1920.

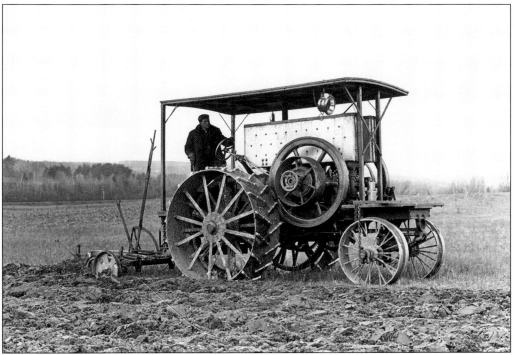

Almost every farm had a gasoline-powered "one lunger" engine for the heavy chores. Abenaque was one of the best; existing machines are highly prized collectors items today. The tractor pictured here is extremely rare.

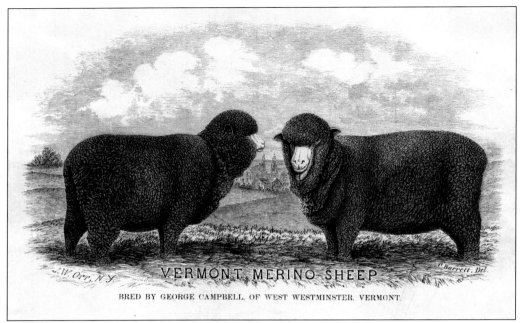

George Campbell of Westminster West took his American merino sheep to exhibit at the International Exhibition in Hamburg, Germany, in 1863. He was awarded first prize for the best ram.

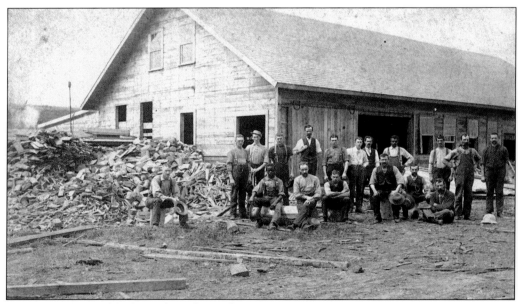

This c. 1890 woodworking shop, located in Westminster Station between the Connecticut River and the railroad, made chair stock. The man sitting on the far left is Henry Wood. Hen Woods Hill Road is named after him.

Three

SAXTONS RIVER

Saxtons River can be described as a small village on a small river. The village and the river have interacted for almost 200 years since the first settlers came to the village in 1783. They were drawn by the three falls that spanned the river, which promised a source of power for the mills that were essential to any settlement. Trees needed to be cut and planed for building houses; corn and wheat needed to be ground for bread; and hides and wool needed to be processed for shoes and clothing.

The story goes that an early surveyor named Saxton had the misfortune of falling into the river, which somehow gave him the honor of having the new village named after him.

The first settlement grew as buildings sprang up along the river. The first school was started at Beaver Dam Hill by Henry Lake in 1795. The Old South Meeting House was built in 1809. The first woolen mill was built in 1815. The first hotel was built by Capt. Jonathan Barron in 1817. The first post office opened in 1818.

Fifty years after the first settlers came, the village was thriving, with the river as its focus. Families came to the area to work in the mills and to farm on the outskirts of the village. The Baptist church started a private high school to educate boys and girls. Social and civic groups were organized to meet the needs of the pre-automobile populace. At the beginning of the 20th century, the population was over 900.

The automobile, the Great Depression, and the world wars all had an impact on life in the village, as young people moved away and sought opportunities in other places. The woolen mill, which had been producing seat covers for Ford cars, burned for the third time in 1939 and was never rebuilt. Then, in 1949, the landmark covered bridge between the upper and middle falls was razed. Life was changing.

Today, the 550 inhabitants of Saxtons River have a new vitality because of their sense of community, sense of place, and fondness for their own history. Hundreds show up for the annual Fourth of July celebration. Restaurants and lodging places attract tourists. Vermont Academy is going strong.

While the village has turned its back on the river as a source of production, it is still tuned in to its hum in the background.

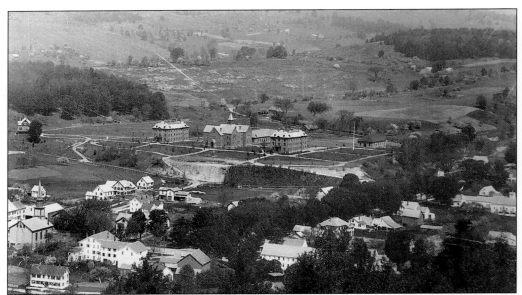

Looking north, this pre-1876 view shows the village of Saxtons River as it appeared before Vermont Academy was built on the hill in the background. The Baptist church (now Christ's Church) is prominent on the left, and the large white building on the right is the Saxwin Building, which housed a tin shop. The Perry home in the center became a tenement and was eventually razed. It is now the site of St. Edmund's Roman Catholic Church.

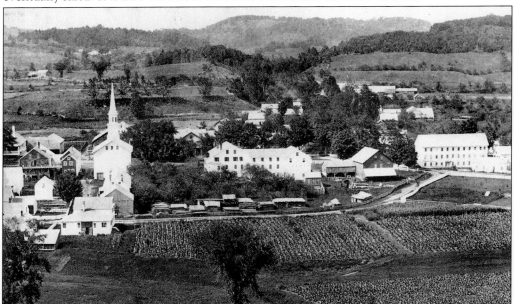

Vermont Academy, founded in 1876, erected dormitories and classroom space on the hill. Seen here are, from left to right, the Sturtevant House, Alumni Hall, Fuller Hall, and Jones Hall, with the dining hall visible behind Fuller Hall and the armory on the far right. The cleared fields attest to the importance of wool in the village economy. The elementary school had not yet been built in the field to the lower left of the academy. The Baptist church is visible in the lower left.

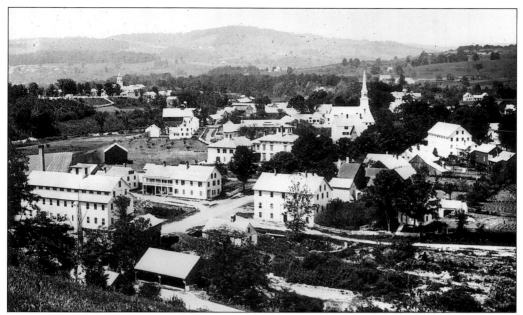

The Saxtons River Worsted Company (far left) occupied a complex at the entrance to the village on the lower falls. Travelers entered the village from the east along the roadway, visible at the bottom of the photograph, and over the covered bridge next to the mill. The building with porches, just past the mill, was a dormitory for workers, and the large building across from it housed offices, wool storage, and the stockroom.

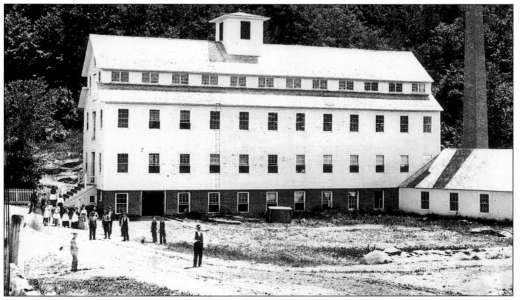

The woolen mill was the village's largest employer. The first mill at this spot was built in 1815. It burned down and was rebuilt twice before burning down for the final time in 1939. It enjoyed its greatest success under the ownership of George Perry, John Farnsworth, and Theophilus Hoit, when it produced wool fabric used for making suits. John F. Alexander (1838–1933) bought the mill from Perry, his father-in-law, in 1866 and continued the operation until 1893.

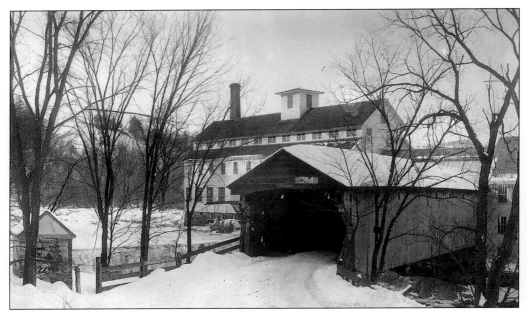

This covered bridge at the entrance to the village was razed in 1899, when the road was rerouted and a new iron arch bridge was erected at the present entrance to the village. The former covered bridge roadbed was used for the trolley lines from 1900 to 1924. A circus advertisement adorns the small building at the left.

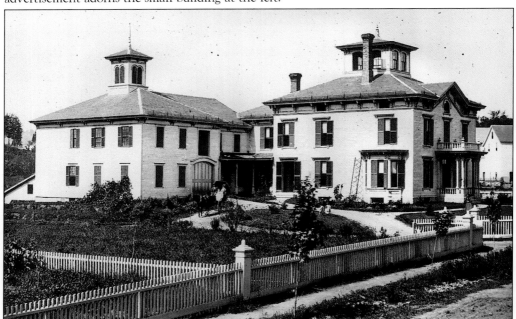

John F. Alexander's success as the owner of the woolen mill is apparent in this large home, which he built just north of the mill. He lived there with his wife, Mary, and children, John, Charlotte, Hannah (called Anna), and George. Anna lived most of her 100 years there. While the mill and boardinghouse are gone, this house remains as a reminder of the grand era of the mill.

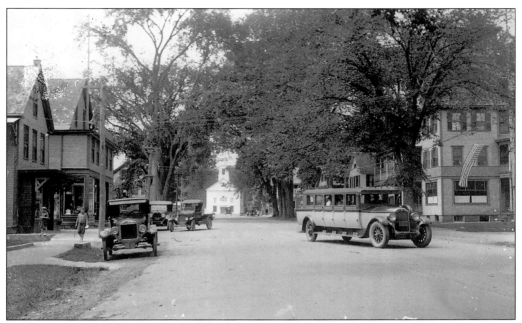

Looking west, this view of Main Street shows an array of vehicles from the 1920s. At the left, in front of the grocery store and Fuller Hardware, are Model T Fords and an early Dodge. A Buick converted to a bus heads east after picking up passengers at the hotel on the right.

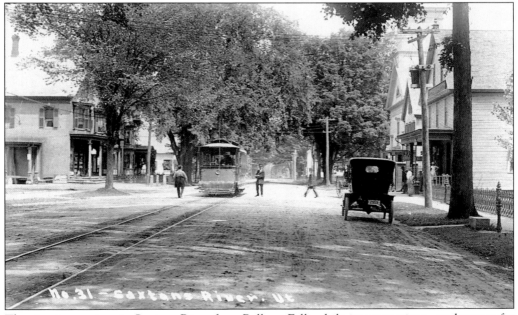

The streetcar arrives in Saxtons River from Bellows Falls while its competitor—and reason for its future demise—is parked at the right. This view looks east, with the Glynn store on the left and Fuller Hardware on the right.

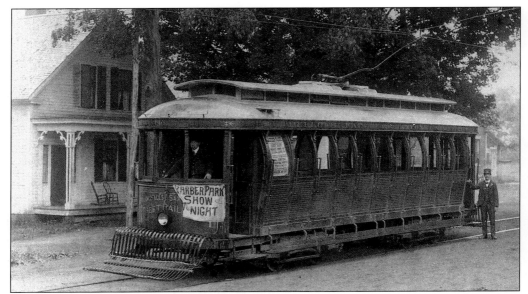

The Bellows Falls and Saxtons River Street Railway operated between those two villages from 1900 to 1924, when it was superseded by the automobile. The line was started as a way to entice passengers to the owners' newly built recreation area, Barber Park, which stood halfway between the two villages. For 5¢, passengers could ride a closed car in winter, or they could ride with the side panels removed in warm weather.

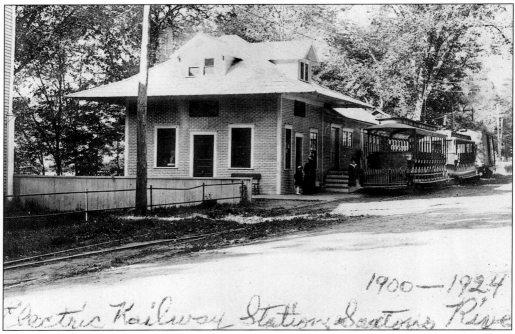

This building served as the ticket office and turnaround point for the street railway. It is currently known as the community building, and an addition houses the Saxtons River Volunteer Fire Department. The streetcars were stored at a carbarn that still stands just north of North Westminster, or Gageville, on the road to Bellows Falls.

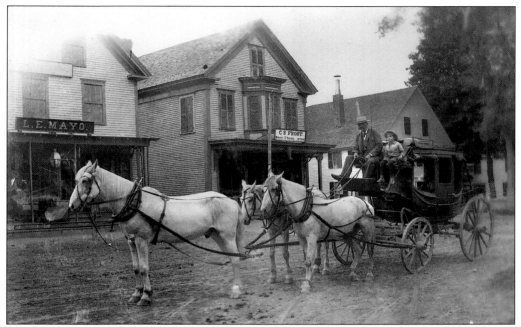

Early transportation in the village took many forms. Note the three-horse hitch on this rig, photographed in front of storefronts on the north side of Main Street. The building to the right of the Frost store is the present site of the telephone company building.

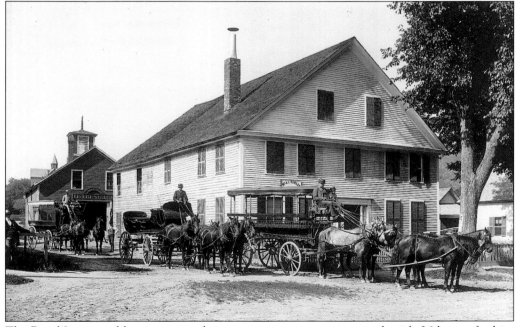

The Rand Livery stable was prepared to meet any transportation need, with 36 horses for hire and 50 to 60 seats on other vehicles available at short notice, from well-upholstered carriages to buckboards with hard bench seating. The large building in front of the livery is Mrs. A.I. Howard's boardinghouse, now the site of the telephone company building.

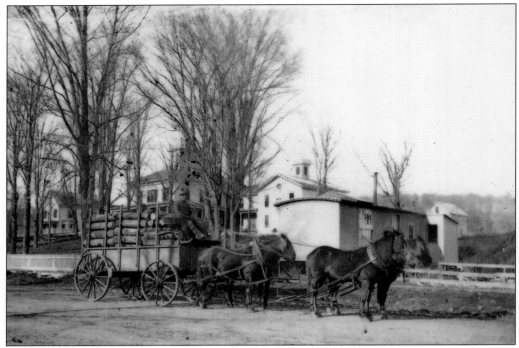

This log load with a four-horse hitch pauses on the west end of Main Street on its way to the lumbermill. In the background is the Scofield House, one of the village's grand houses that was moved from Cambridgeport but razed in 1960 after years of neglect. Frank Taft's portable photography studio is seen behind the horses.

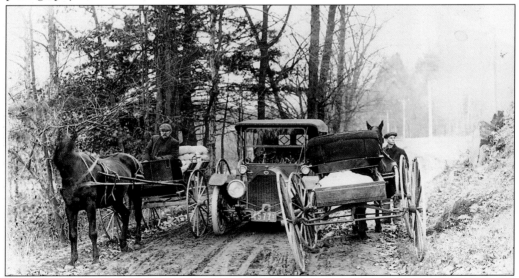

The beginning of one era and the end of another met on a muddy road in 1916 when Walter Glynn's automobile collided with Dorr Moses Thayer's buggy on the Barber Park Road. Thayer, a granite and marble merchant and close friend of Glynn, sued the prominent businessman and won. In turn, Thayer was sued by the streetcar company for damages caused by his runaway horse, which collided with one of its cars.

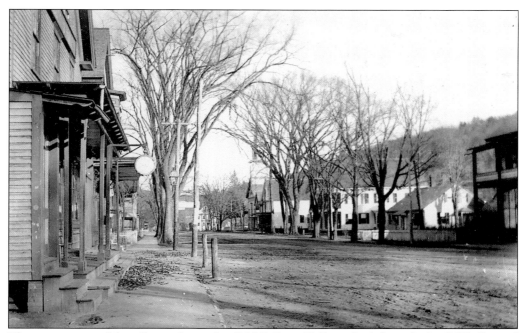

This view east on Main Street shows the Odd Fellows Hall on the left, with the C.W. Osgood barbershop and jewelry store beyond. Note the large watch sign. The building on the right, known as the Frost Block, once housed the post office, a jewelry store, a restaurant, and the First National store. It was destroyed by fire in 1979.

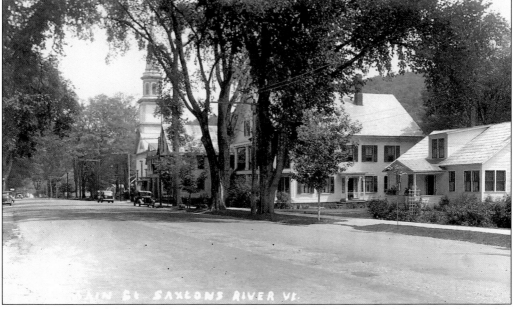

Except for the model year of the vehicles in the street and the overarching elms, this earlier view of the south side of Main Street, looking east, appears much the same as it does today. The large structure is the Colvin House, and the Baptist church (now Christ's Church) is visible in the background.

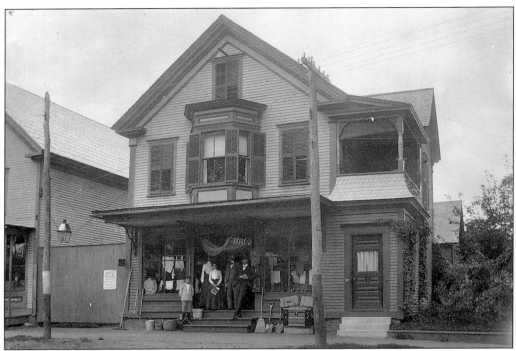
The Warners operated a dry goods store at this site on the north side of Main Street.

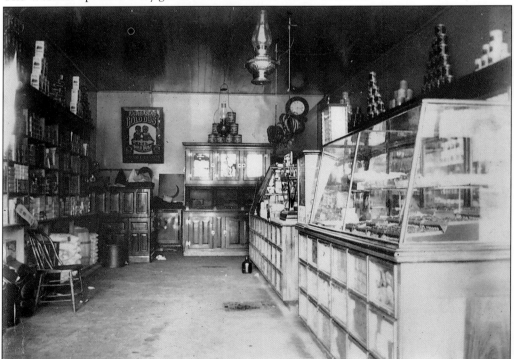
The Warners' store carried a full array of items essential to life in a small 19th-century Vermont village.

The Odd Fellows Hall on Main Street served many purposes. Commercial activity on the first floor included C.W. Osgood's store, which sold watches, jewelry, and optical goods and served as a barbershop. Note the barber pole on the left-hand storefront. The door on the left opened onto the stairway to the second floor, where the International Order of Odd Fellows held its meetings and community members gathered for plays, concerts, donkey basketball, and voting.

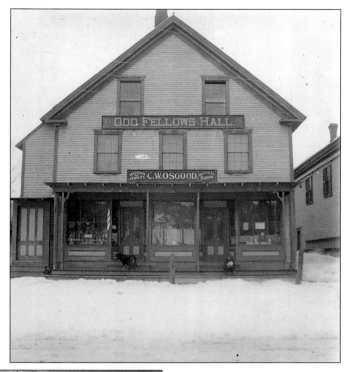

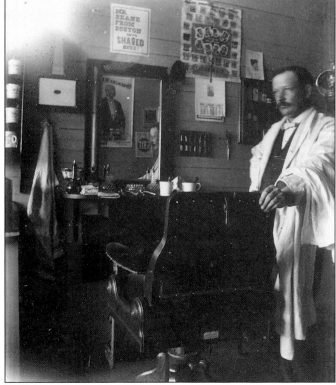

Charlie Osgood's barber chair was always busy as gentlemen spiffed up for Saturday night or a trip to Bellows Falls. The building also housed a pool hall in a back room.

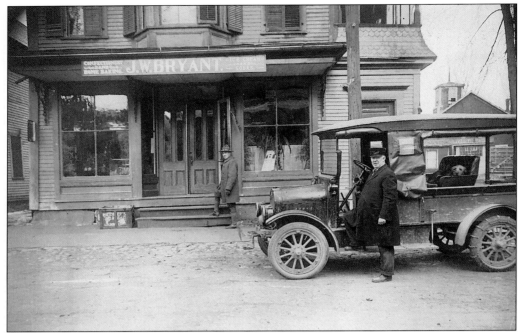

Jack Bryant's ice-cream parlor took over the Warner store space on Main Street. Bryant and his dog are pictured here, with Arthur Thompson in his World War I uniform about to sample Bryant's wares. Bryant advertised, "Confectionery and Home Baking." Thompson was one of at least 27 Saxtons River men who served in the war, including one who died and many who suffered early deaths due to wounds and poison gas.

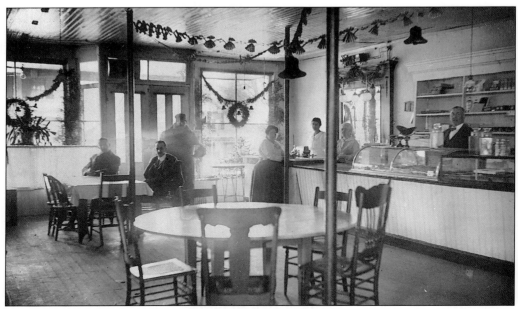

Jack Bryant stands behind the counter of his ice-cream parlor.

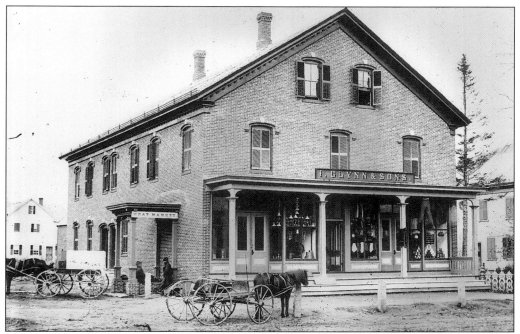

The window of the I. Glynn & Sons store on Main Street features artfully displayed kerosene lamp shades, canned goods, and clothing. The two men on the left wait to have their delivery off-loaded at the meat market while a horse stands tied to a granite hitching post. Much of the merchandise has changed, but the store continues today as an important part of the village's mercantile and social life.

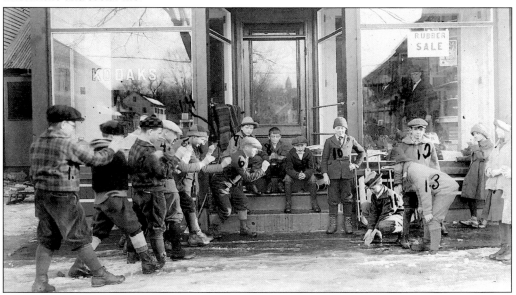

On a February day in 1925, a group of village boys gathers to play marbles in front of Fuller Hardware on Main Street. They are, from left to right, John Bevan, John Snarski, John Lawrence, Edward Freeman, Henry Kinney, Stanley Snarski, Earl Simonds, Paul Colvin, Walter Walker, Harold LaClair, Lawrence Austin, Lewis Austin, Lawrence Moore, and Alvah Buxton.

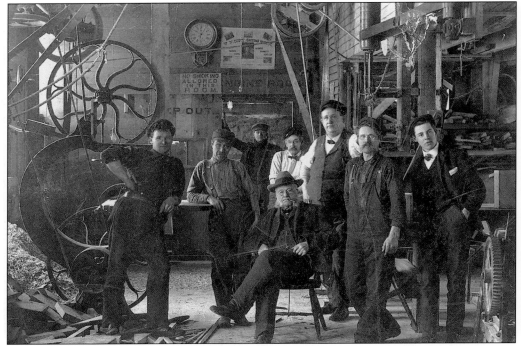

W.W. Cory owned a blacksmith and carriage shop that stood behind Fuller Hardware on Main Street. This photograph was taken c. 1882, before the business was bought and moved to Bellows Falls.

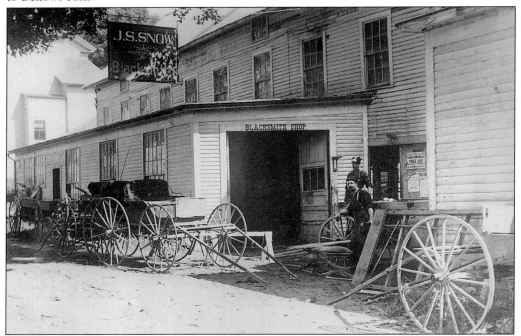

The J.S. Snow blacksmith and carriage-making shop was in business behind the Baptist church (now Christ's Church) off River Street in what is now the church's parking lot.

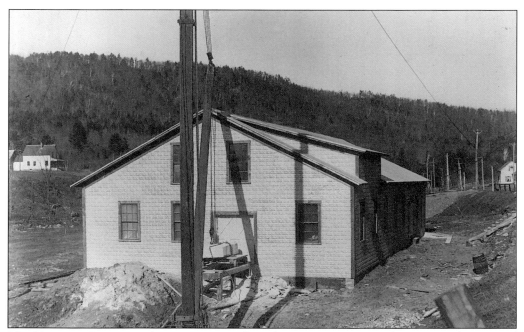

The Vermont Soapstone Corporation stood on the Saxtons River at the corner of Main and Oak Streets. It cut and polished the soapstone that was mined in Cambridgeport and Grafton. It was an important early industry in the area. The firm was sold at auction in 1910.

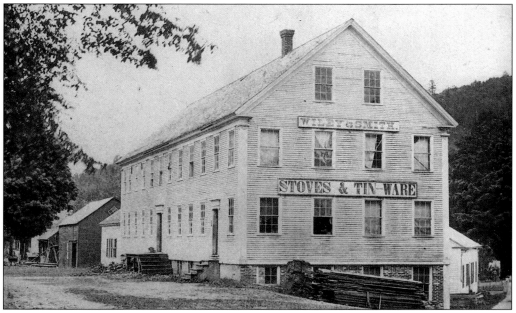

The Wiley & Smith tin shop, at the corner of Main and Maple Streets, produced a wide variety of tin objects. More than 30 itinerant salesmen peddled their wares from carts to area farmers in the 1860s. This building has gone through many transformations over the years. It has served as a paint factory, telephone company, photography studio, grocery store, frozen food locker, plumbing shop, and antique shop. It currently houses a number of small businesses.

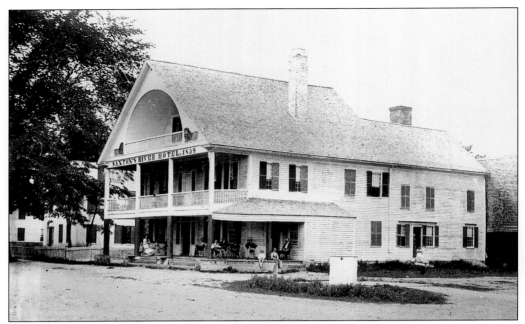

The Saxton's River Hotel was completed in 1859 by owner Abel K. Wilder, who painted the lions on the front. A hotel had stood at the site as early as 1817, when Capt. Jonathan Barron, an early settler and landowner, began construction.

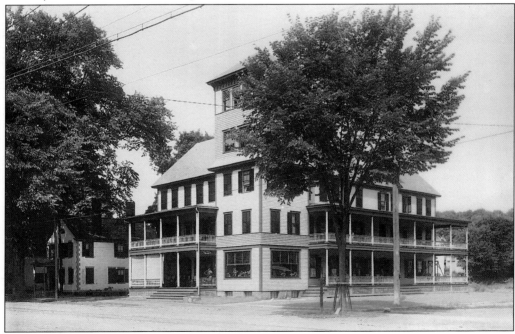

The 1859 Saxton's River Hotel was replaced by this structure in 1903. Economist Maj. L.L.B. Angas, who owned the building in the 1960s, used to shoot golf balls into a net on the second-floor side porch until its collapse. Other than the loss of the porch, the structure appears the same to this day and operates under the name of the Inn at Saxtons River.

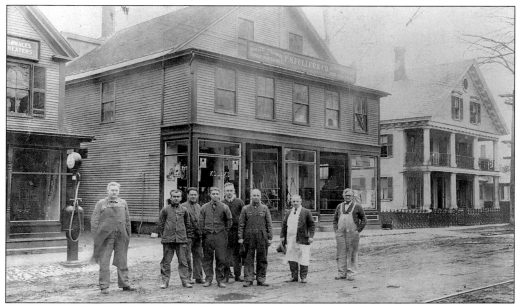

Employees of F.S. Fuller Hardware Store and two of the village's other shopkeepers pose on Main Street. They are, from left to right, ? Kemp, a shoemaker; David Stearns, Robert O'Conner, Harry Adams, Bill Wright, and Fred Freeman, Fuller employees; Fred Simonds, a grocer; and Fay Fuller, owner of the hardware store behind them.

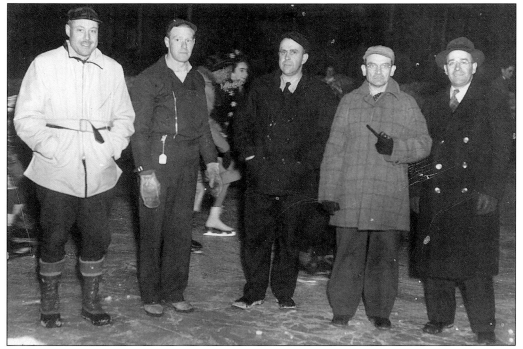

These well-known Saxtons River men served on the skating-rink committee of the civic association in 1942. They are, from left to right, Elisha "Caesar" Camp, Philip Frey, Larry Burgess, Humphrey B. Neill, and Robert O'Connor.

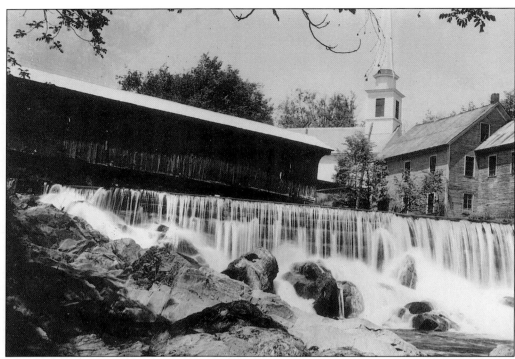

An attraction for early settlers in Saxtons River was the waterpower available from three dams along the river—the upper, middle, and lower falls. A covered bridge spanned the river just above the middle falls. Known as the Saw Mill Bridge, it was razed in 1949.

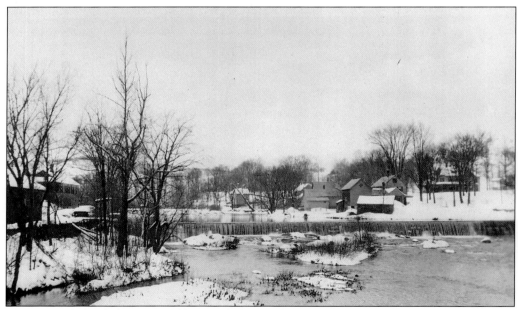

The waters behind the upper falls provided a fondly remembered skating pond in the winter. These falls powered the saws at the Thompson lumbermill.

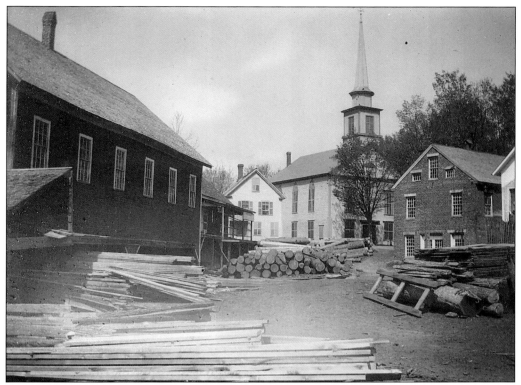

Several mills were powered by the middle falls, including this lumbermill that later became known as Frey's Mill. A blacksmith shop occupied the brick building, and a house stood between the former Congregational church (now the Saxtons River Historical Society Museum) and the river. Only the church exists today.

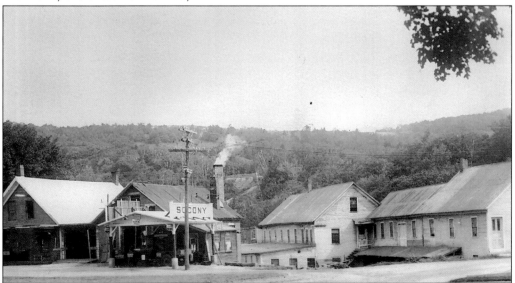

Frey's Mill and the gas station are seen from the corner of Main and Westminster Streets. The mill complex burned in 1959, leaving only traces of the foundations.

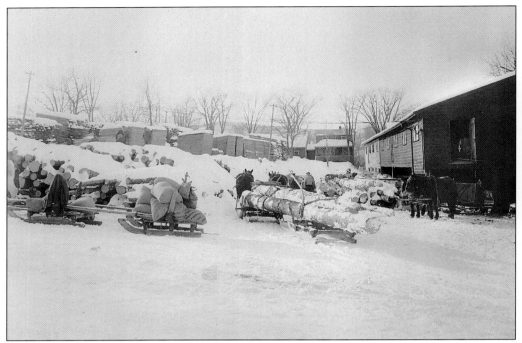

Mills were located on the upper falls on the west side of Westminster Street, next to the covered bridge, beginning in 1814. In 1892, Henry Thompson began a sawmill operation here that continues as a lumberyard today. This is a view of the mill yard in winter with a sledload of grain and feed, a sledload of logs, and a sled at the sawdust-loading chute. The Thompsons also ran a gristmill at this site.

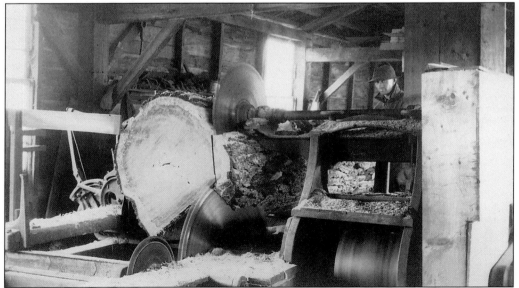

Lew Thompson took over the operation of the mill from his father in 1920 and ran it until he sold the mill to Claude Tenney in 1946. Thompson is pictured here, behind the mill's over-and-under saws.

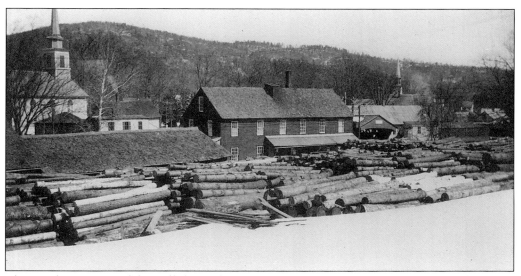

This northwest view of the mill shows the extent of the operation. Note the covered bridge in the background.

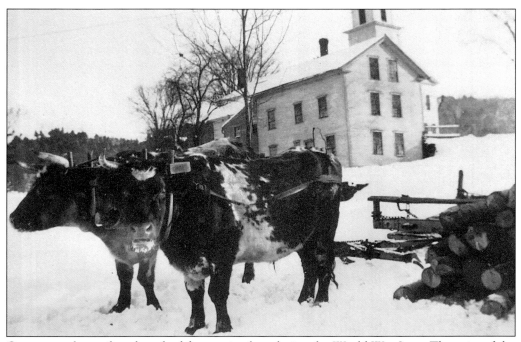

Oxen were the preferred method for moving logs during the World War I era. The spire of the Old South Meeting House peeks from behind a nearby house on Westminster Street.

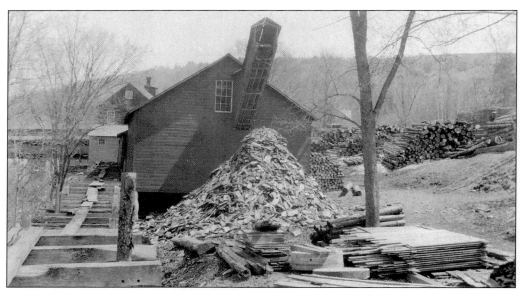

This view, looking east, shows the Thompson sawmill and the slab carrier and slab pile below it. On the left is the top of the flume structure that carried the water from the river through the mills to power the machinery.

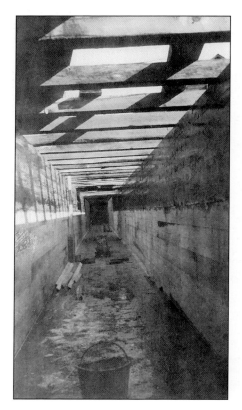

This is a view of the flume from below when it was emptied and awaiting repairs. The flume ran along the rear of the mill, carrying water to the wheels powering both the gristmill and sawmill.

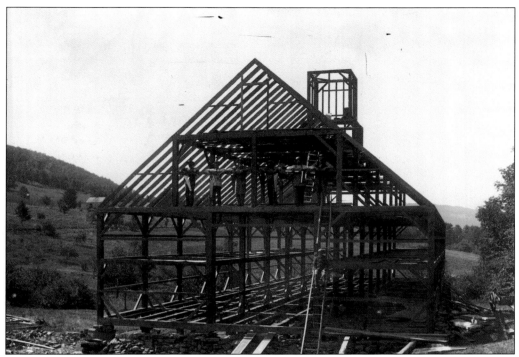

These workers pause for a photograph while constructing a barn the old-fashioned way at a farm just outside the village. The barn and all of the buildings except the house and one storage shed burned to the ground on August 12, 1957. The farm was once owned by the Fancy and Pruden families.

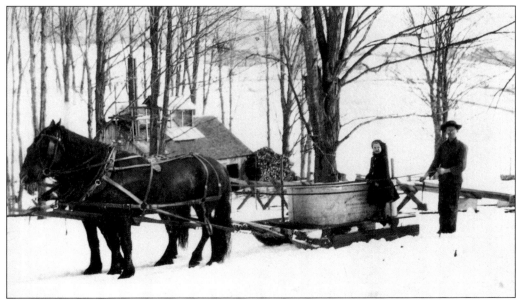

Gathering maple sap was a family affair on the John Fancy farm. The horses pulled the sledge through the woods while the sap gatherers emptied the buckets into the large metal tub. The sap was boiled for syrup in the sugarhouse visible in the background.

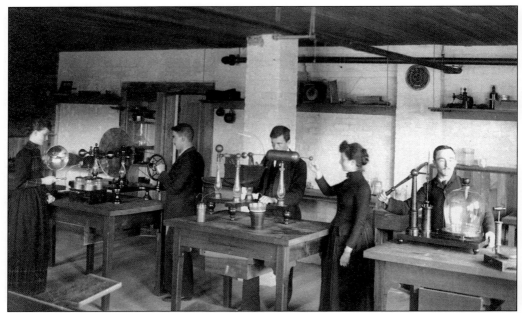

Vermont Academy was founded in 1876 by the state Baptist association as a high school for boys and girls, offering a classical or scientific education. Economic and other considerations forced out the girls at some point in the school's history, but today they enjoy full status among the 250-member student body. (Courtesy of Vermont Academy.)

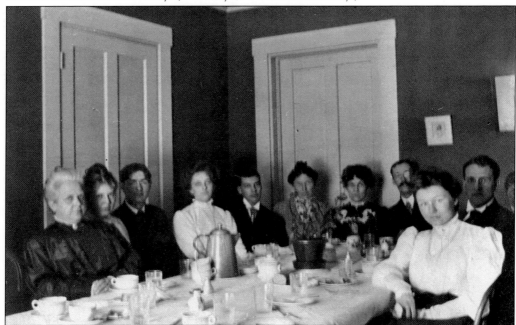

A group of Vermont Academy teachers gathers for coffee and dessert c. 1906. They are, from left to right, Harriet Moor, Adelaide F. True (the lady principal), Charles C. Tillinghast (after whom the library is named), Homer E. Hunt (Class of 1902), Roxane Tuttle, Alice B. Files, Clarence B. Hill, Anna M.Wilson, ? Winsor, and Florence Ellery.

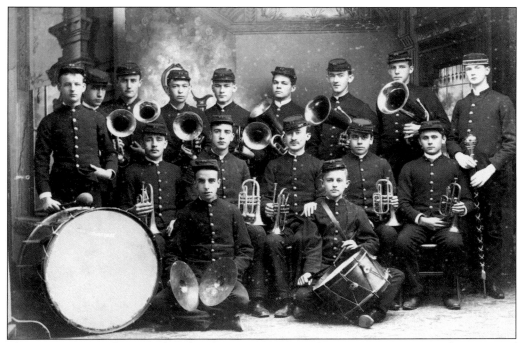
The Vermont Academy student band poses c. 1888. Military maneuvers were also a part of academy life.

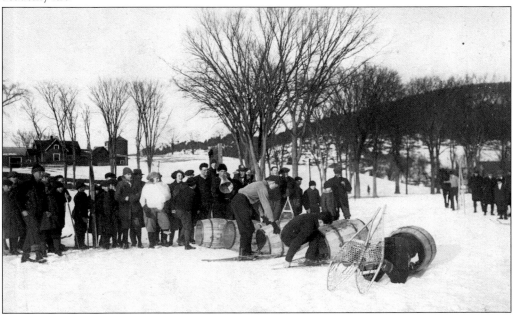
In 1909, James Taylor, assistant headmaster at Vermont Academy, founded the Green Mountain Club and organized the first winter sports carnival on snow in New England, predating the Dartmouth Winter Carnival by a year. Taylor is also credited with conceiving the idea of Vermont's Long Trail. Students here run an obstacle course that requires them to pass through barrels on skis and snowshoes. The academy's winter carnival tradition continues today.

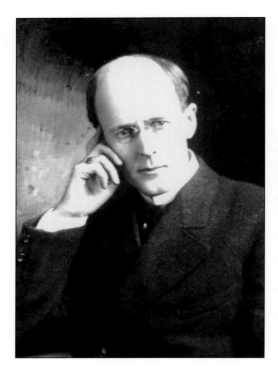

Paul Harris (1868–1947) was one of a number of notable Vermont Academy students. A prominent lawyer in Chicago, he founded Rotary International in 1905. Harris was raised by his grandparents in Wallingford, and he had a checkered academic career until finding his calling. Although he had been dismissed by the University of Vermont for a prank, he was awarded an honorary doctor of laws by the university for his later work with Rotary International and other civic organizations. (Courtesy of Rotary International Archives.)

Florence Sabin (1871–1953) was noted for several firsts for women in the field of medicine, including being the first named a full professor at Johns Hopkins, the first elected to the National Academy of Sciences, and the first elected president of the American Association of Anatomists. Her research led to important discoveries about tuberculosis and the origin of the lymphatic system. Although she was born and brought up in Colorado, her family roots were in Saxtons River, and she lived with her grandparents while attending Vermont Academy.

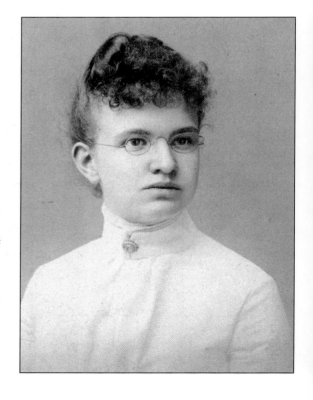

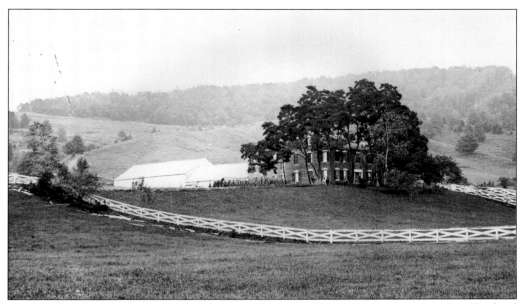

In 1895, Sarah Warner deeded her farm and home on Westminster Street to New England Kurn Hattin Homes to be used as a home and school for boys who were not able to live with their families for a variety of reasons. The Warner Home opened in 1898 with eight boys and a matron.

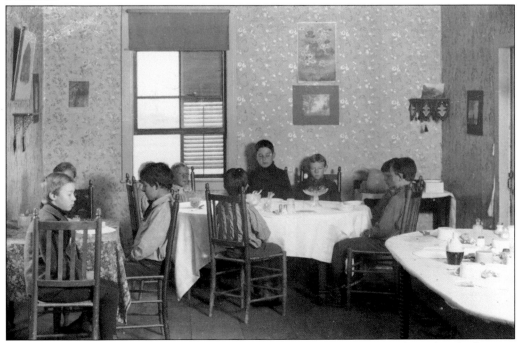

The boys at the Warner Home shared family-style meals, dining on produce they had grown themselves. In 1922, the boys were moved to the Westminster campus, and the Warner Home was opened to girls. Both campuses were consolidated in Westminster in 1993, and the former Warner Home became an incubator business center.

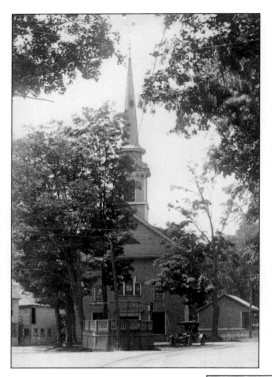

The Congregationalists built this church in 1836 because of dissension among the Baptists, Congregationalists, and Universalists who shared the Old South Meeting House. This view shows the bandstand that once stood at the intersection. In 1966, the historical society, with Kenneth Morrison as its first president, founded a museum here.

A group of onlookers gathers to watch the installation of the bell in the Baptist church on Main Street. The church was built in 1840. In 1936, the Baptist and Congregationalist churches federated, forming Christ's Church and alternating services between the two buildings.

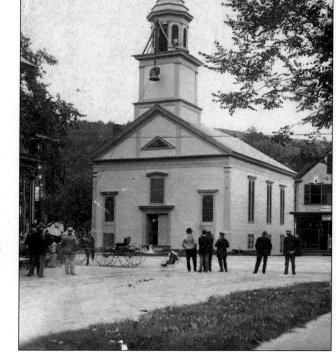

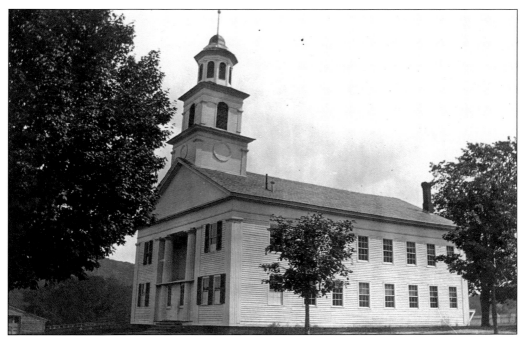

The Old South Meeting House stood at the entrance to the cemetery from 1809 to 1974, when it was razed and a park was created and dedicated to the memory of Dr. Frederick L. Osgood. Over the years, the building served as a place of worship, a community gathering place, a private seminary (1842–1866), a public school (1875–1915, when the current elementary school was built), and a place of worship for Baptists, Congregationalists, Universalists, and Roman Catholics.

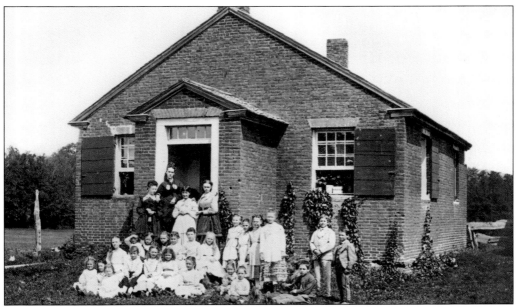

The Beaver Dam Schoolhouse on the Westminster West Road is now a private residence next to the Saxtons River Playhouse.

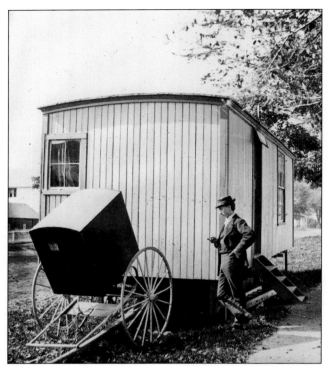

Frank Taft (1851–1938) was a member of a prolific family of photographers that included his father, Preston, and brother Edward (Ned). Frank took many photographs of everyday life in Saxtons River and Bellows Falls, using this portable darkroom in his travels. His office, pictured here, was located on Main Street across the alley from the Odd Fellows Hall (now home to Main Street Arts).

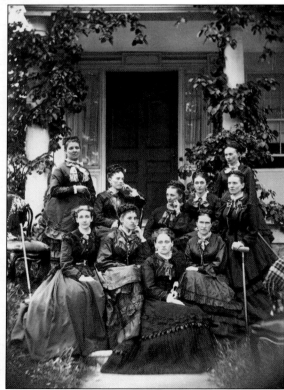

Croquet players pose for Taft in their finest, giving us a glimpse of the hair and dress styles of the day.

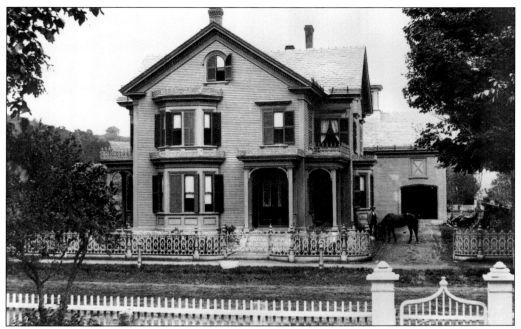

Taft photographed most of the buildings on Main Street, providing a valuable historical record. The John and Mary Jane Farnsworth house, on the north side of the street, looks much the same today except for the absence of the elaborate wrought-iron fence. The fence in the foreground bordered the Perry house, which was the site of the first Vermont Academy classes. It later burned and is now the site of St. Edmund's Roman Catholic Church, built in 1952.

Taft did a brisk business in photographing locals, using ornate painted backdrops and props for a bucolic effect. Among the subjects here are Carrie Bancroft Neill and James Bancroft. The gentleman in the center is clowning for the camera by twirling his hat on his foot.

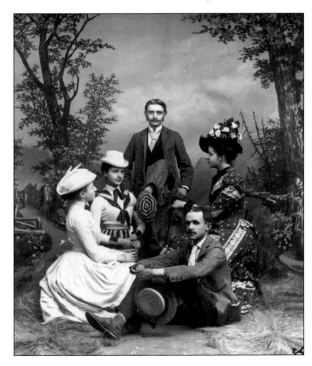

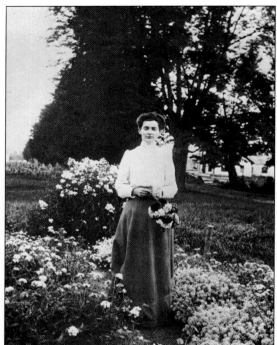

Lena Osgood Long (1871–1967) lived in Saxtons River from 1926 until her death. While a young woman in East Pittsford, she spent 15 years photographing her neighbors at work on their farms, sugaring, cutting wood, and enjoying the pleasures of rural life. Between 1900 and 1905, she captured on 83 glass plates the construction of the new Chittenden and East Pittsford dams.

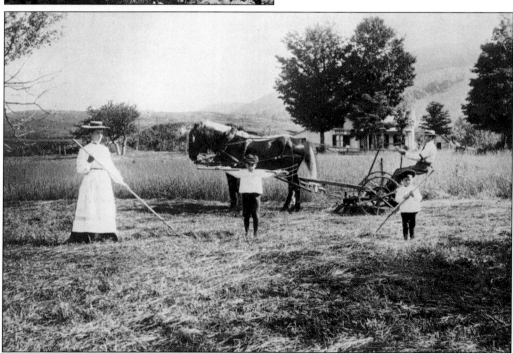

Lena Osgood Long captured this scene of rural life, showing Rosie and Harley Perkins and their two sons on their farm in East Pittsford. After her marriage to Arthur Long in 1908, Lena seems to have given up photography. A cache of 353 mounted photographs and 228 glass plates was discovered in her home after her death.

Julia Ann Clarke (1815–1906) and her brother Albert Clarke (1817–1897) were descendants of one of the first families to settle in the area. Their father, Timothy Clarke, bought land from Colonel Bellows of Walpole, New Hampshire, and cleared it before Vermont became an independent state and while it was still under the jurisdiction of the state government of New York. The property just north of Saxtons River remained in the Clarke family until it was sold to the Shepard family in 1943.

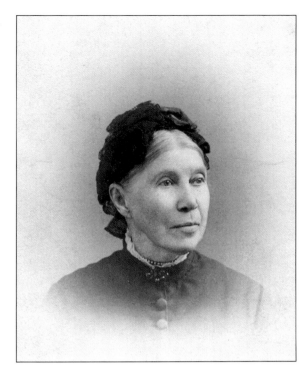

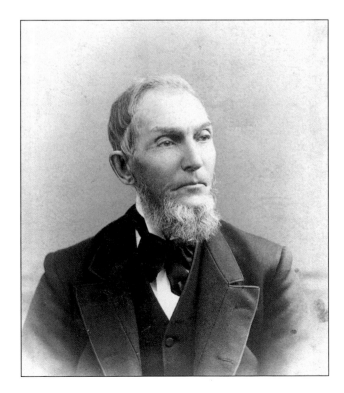

Albert Clark was one of 10 children. He and his wife, Ann, had three children: Charles, who became a prominent dentist in Bellows Falls; Harriet, who was a well-known singer in the Boston area; and Joseph, who remained to run the farm and care for his aged parents and aunts.

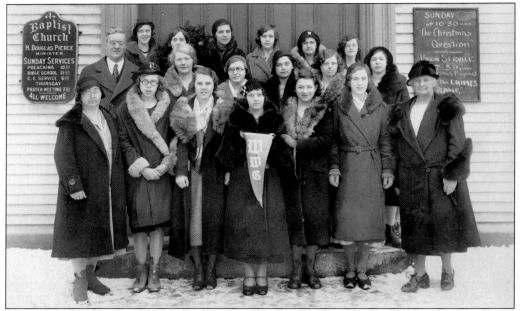

The World Wide Guild of the Baptist church is pictured here. They are, from left to right, as follows: (front row) Ethel Cole, Josephine Patnode Glynn, Dorothy Adams Knowlton, Dorothy Clayton, Mercedes Tarbell, Sylvia Rumney, and May Hatfield; (middle row) Rev. H.D. Pierce (pastor of the church), Helen Beals Freitas, Ruth Clayton, Nellie Townsend Stevens, Lola Hastings, and Wilma Wright Thurber; (back row) Eileen Pierce Townsend, Clara Parker Aldrich, Hazel Stevens, Marjory Beals Patch, Madeline Clayton, and Thelma Cole Daigneault.

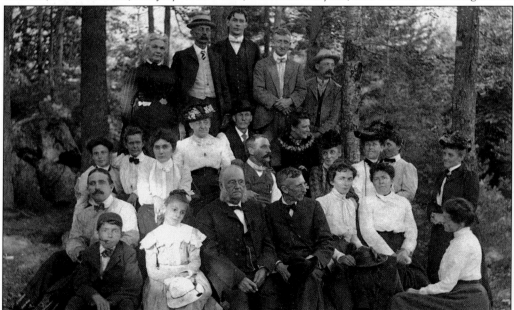

This group hiked and picnicked on the Vermont Academy grounds one Fourth of July c. 1900. In the front row are, from left to right, Joseph Machado, Alice Scofield (later Kelly), Lewis Tenney, unidentified, Edith White, Mrs. William Corey, and Grace Chapin. The others are unidentified.

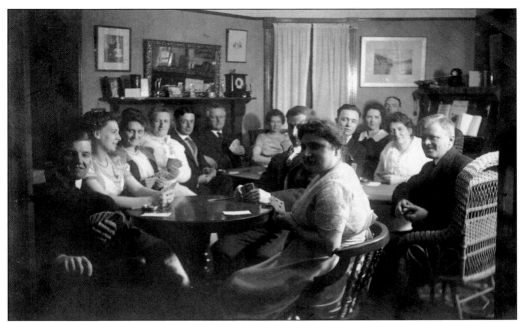

The Young Adult Group meets to play cards in 1918. They are, from left to right, Jim Kelley, Alice Kelley, Blanche Hughes, ? Alexander, Alex Campbell, George Alexander, Deborah Colvin, George Buxton, Ora Campbell, Floyd Bowen, Nell Buxton, Cecil Hughes, Josephine Bowen, and Paul Colvin. Colvin, the son of Deborah Cory Colvin, died during World War II.

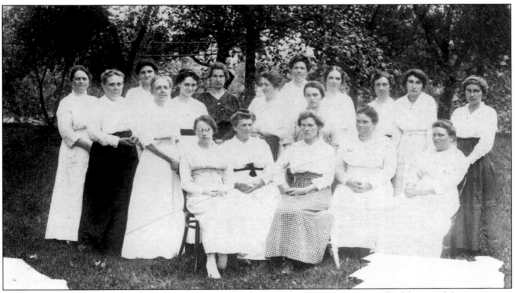

The Nature Club was founded in 1903 to study nature. It continues to hold monthly meetings to this day, although it has a broader social agenda. Seen here are, from left to right, the following: (front row) ? Woodlock, May Hatfield, Fanny Pettengill, Cora Fuller, and Carrie Dillingham; (back row) Katharine Glynn (the club's first secretary), Mrs. Austin Farr, Mary Buchanan, Minnie Spaulding, Blanche Hughes, Deborah Colvin, Josephine Bowen, Grace Chapin, Margret Abbott, Nell Buxton, Nina Davis, Mrs. Benjamin Hall, and Harriet Wright.

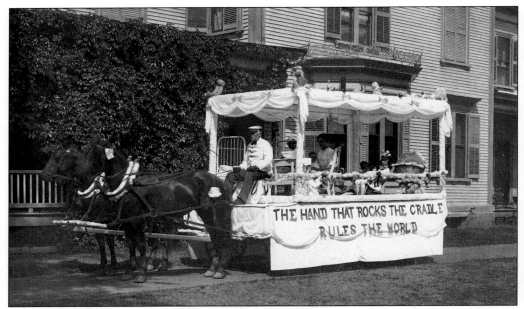

This Mothers Club entry in the Fourth of July parade made a statement about the importance of women in the life of the village's children. The tradition of the Fourth of July parade and celebration continues in the village today.

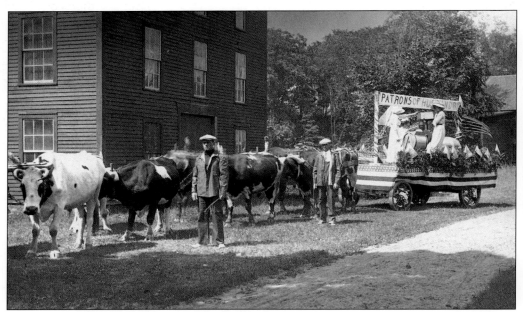

The Patrons of Husbandry used a team of oxen, a butter churn, and a pair of milkmaids to make a point about the importance of agriculture. The building in the background, built on the north side of the river in 1870, served as a tannery for 20 years. Here, fur was removed from animal pelts before they were processed into leather for the village's carriage, harness, and boot makers. The building is still standing.

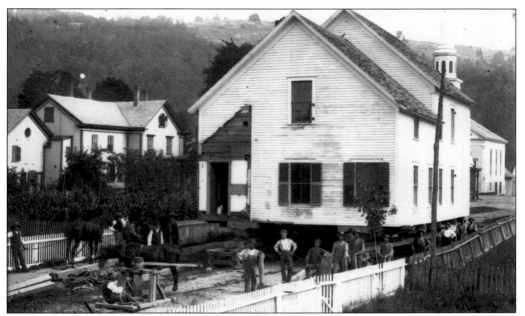

The crew stops for a photograph while undertaking the enormous task of moving a house up Academy Avenue. Note the horse and capstan used to move the building along on wooden cribs.

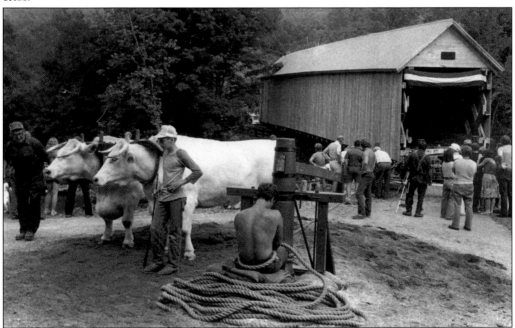

Less than 100 years later, in 1982, the same technique was used—this time using the oxen, Duke and Dan, driven by Anne Ruth Pearce—to pull a new covered bridge into place under the direction of master bridge builder Arnold Graton (far left) and his sons. The original 1867 Hall Covered Bridge, which crossed the river east of the village, had collapsed two years before under the weight of an overloaded truck. (Courtesy of Jack Peters.)

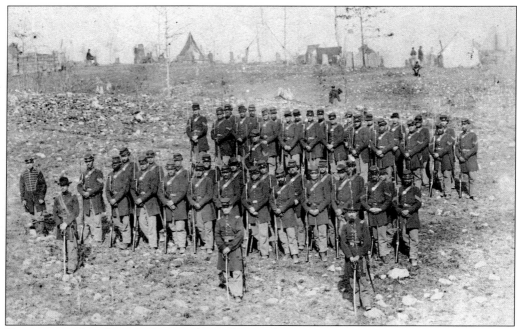

Vermonters played a significant role in the Civil War. Company I, 12th Vermont, poses at Wolf Shoals in Virginia in 1862. Many Saxtons River men were part of this unit. Rockingham sent 243 men to the war, of whom 24 did not return. Capt. Franklin George Butterfield of Saxtons River received the Medal of Honor for his valiant actions at Salem Heights, Virginia.

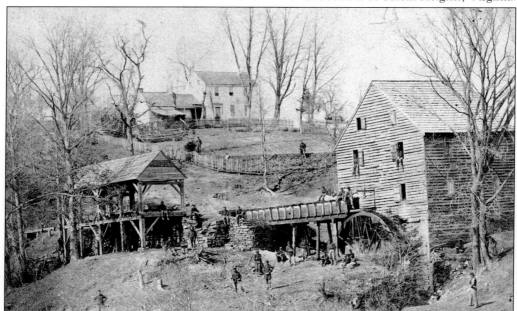

The boys of Company I, 12th Vermont, do their washing during a stop at the Ford property in Wolf Shoals, Virginia. Ford's sawmill (left) and gristmill provide an idyllic setting that belies the tragedy of the war. After the war, many young men who had never been away from home before answered the call of the movement west.